Cape Town

Apartheid – its effects
and its ending

To dear Geoff and Pat
what memories! !
love
    Pam and Gordan

Cape Town Stories:

Apartheid – its effects and its ending

GORDON GADDES

THE CHOIR PRESS

First published in the United Kingdom in 2016 by
The Choir Press

ISBN 978-1-910864-44-9

Contents

⤳⤳⤳

Preface

⌒⌒⌒

This book is dedicated to the people of Langa Township in Cape Town, and to Pam Gaddes, who has encouraged me at every stage in our Cape Town journey and who passed away on 23 June 2015. Pam and I first visited Langa in November 2010 on a tour which included calling in on the Dalukhanyo Pre-School. We, along with other tourists in our group, were deeply moved by the energy and the joy in the faces of the young children who greeted and danced for us. Coming from the UK we felt humbled to find this human spirit in the township situation. Over dinner that evening Pam and I decided that we could and should do more than 'just put some money in the tourists' collection box in the pre-school'. Three months later we established the Langa Township Pre-School Trust (LTPT). Over the next five years we made four visits to Cape Town, spending a total of eighteen weeks in the area, and I am here again in October 2015, Cape Town's spring time.

These stories and vignettes have arisen following our experiences in the Cape Town area, which triggered questions that we wanted to try to answer. Each story carries its own message, but all the stories hang together in their focus. They are reflections and comments on persons, areas and happenings in the Cape Town area especially during apartheid and through to now, capturing the struggle and showing progress during the recent democratic period. Our relatives and friends ask questions, wanting facts, impressions and conclusions, searching for the truth of things just as we do. The stories try to bring to the reader subjects chosen and researched by me, which will interest the Friends of the Langa Township Pre-School Trust and perhaps a wider audience. They rely heavily on material drawn from a wide variety of sources as acknowledged in the bibliography. The vignettes are mostly short writings, whimsical and evocative pieces arising during the stay here.

I would like to thank Rob Small of Harvest for Hope for his advice and encouragement concerning two of the stories, and the Rev. Canon Rodney Whiteman for his wise counsel, and Clarence Mahamba and the Ladies of Dalukhanyo for their help and understanding as I probed into their lives for two of the Langa stories. Finally, a thank you to Jeff Wallis, who has helped at every stage with advice on publishing, design and layout and has acted as a critical friend, and to our daughter Sarah Pickles for helping me with some of the 'technical' aspects.

My tribute overleaf is to Pam, my soul mate for fifty-eight years and, as Denis Healey said about his wife, 'my better half', with thanks for the love, wisdom and support she has given me.

This book is dedicated also to the people of Langa as a tribute to them for the endurance and courage that they have shown over the decades, and to thank them for the openness, friendship and courtesy with which they have received us as we have moved among them from time to time. Maybe we are being naive, but we have not felt the fear that some people seem to attach to township visits and I am reminded of the saying that 'there is nothing to fear but fear itself'. So this introduction ends in sharing with you the concluding sentence of Malcolm Lesiter's piece 'One Day in Langa Township', following our visit to Langa with our wives on 6 November 2012, Malcolm writing: 'What a day! Our eyes and hearts were opened and more than once our mouths gaped.'

Gordon Gaddes, Fish Hoek, Cape Town, 29 October 2015

An Appreciation of
Pam Gaddes JP, Cert. Ed.

೧೧೧

Pam was born in Sheffield but spent most of her early years in Welling-borough. Her later education was at Wellingborough High School and Homerton College, Cambridge. She was married to Gordon for nearly fifty-seven years, meeting him at a 'Conservative Coming-up Dance' at the Red Lion in Cambridge in October 1957, odd in a sense because they were both left of centre! She was mother to Sarah and Jim, sister to Sue and grandmother to Sam, Fergus, Ben and Florence Pickles and to Faye, Emily, Sophia and Luca Gaddes.

Pam lived in Hemel Hempstead for fifty years, five years in Highfield and forty-five years in Adeyfield, despite thinking that the stay there might be for only two years. She was a junior school teacher over forty years, in Wellingborough, Cambridge and Peterborough and finally in Hemel Hempstead at Belswains and Maylands junior schools, and then for eleven years at Aycliffe Drive where also she was a teacher governor. She was a founder group tutor for the Dacorum Adult Literacy Campaign. She was an inspiring teacher – when she was nineteen, at the end of three summer weeks of temporary teaching in a Wellingborough junior school, the Head described her as 'a most reliable and conscientious teacher' who 'conducted and marked end of term tests most efficiently', whilst her 'playing the piano was a great help in assembly' and she produced 'delightful musical items at the end of term concert', and 'her enthusiasm and special ability in teaching PE was an inspiration to the children'.

Pam was heavily involved in our community, serving as an SDP borough councillor for Cupid Green, as a Dacorum magistrate for twelve years, as chairman and then president of Relate for fifteen years, as chair of the Hemel Hempstead Anglican Deanery, chair of the Hemel Hempstead and Berkhamsted Deaneries Social Responsibility Committee, and as a church warden at St Paul's Church, Highfield. She was involved in the start-up of two nursery play groups and was a member of the 'DENS Future' Working Party, which established the long-term future of the Dacorum Emergency Night Shelter for the homeless,

and a founder trustee of the Langa Township Pre-School Trust, supporting young township children in Cape Town.

Pam had many loves, her family and friends foremost, and also classical
and church music and jazz, travel at home and abroad, and reading. Her
games enthusiasms included watching cricket, golf and rugby, and earlier,
as a player, hockey, tennis, squash, golf and skiing. She loved entertaining
at her hospitable Highfield Lane home, where she passed away peacefully
on 23 June, following a long stay in Watford and Hammersmith hospitals.

Gordon Gaddes, Hemel Hempstead, 27 June 2015

Pam Gaddes, Rosas, Spain, August 2008

Introduction

～⌒～

The stories have been arranged into four parts, each part having its own theme.

Part I covers **the apartheid period** and includes a description of apartheid, its roots and its effects. Also included are two stories focusing on the 'forced removals', respectively in District Six and Simon's Town. Finally in this part we consider two major influences on the dismantling of apartheid, the story of the role of the faith groups and that of sport.

Part II focuses on **the Flats**, the story 'The Cape Flats' being followed by 'Langa Township' and 'An Unsung Hero'. Concluding this part there is 'A Day in Langa Township', an appreciation by the Venerable Reverend Malcolm Lesiter.

Part III, '**Rainbow Signs**', looks forward and is about co-operation between the ethnic groups of the rainbow nation and the encouragement of self-help. The stories cover micro-farming initiatives, the role of people as leaders and team builders, co-operation in the Winelands, and examples of major welfare and educational initiatives led by philanthropists and churches.

Part IV includes the **vignettes**, which are evocative pieces of varying lengths carrying special memories.

The **epilogues** have been produced variously. Fergus Pickles, our grandson, has reviewed all of the stories and vignettes and considered them in the light of his deep experience of the Johannesburg area during several months in the summer of 2014. It seemed to me a good idea to include reflections from another source, a person half a century younger than me and able to introduce different perspectives. The second piece is by Nadia Petersen, who lives in Ocean View, Cape Town, and is a cry from the heart, which I could not resist including in the form in which I received it by e-mail. My only comment on it at this stage is that the roots of apartheid went back three centuries in the attitudes, policies and actions of the settlers.

Each story tries to understand and to explain; the interpretations are very personal, but I have tried to be objective and truthful. Of course the philosopher will say that 'truth' is a very tricky concept and that what is truthful is in the eye of the beholder and, moreover, that the very words one chooses to describe something involve a bias. For this reason it has been important to refer to leaders, writers and authorities to illustrate the stories, but I stand personally by the judgements made in the selection of the stories and the interpretations and conclusions that may be drawn from these.

Gordon Gaddes, Skilpadvlei (Tortoise Valley) Wine Farm, Stellenbosch,
8 November 2015

Part I

The Apartheid Period

In his preface to Father Cosmas Desmond's book, The Discarded People, *Lord Caradon stated:*

'This is a terrifying book. It is the account of callous contempt for human suffering, the ugliness of systematic cruelty, and the self-righteousness of the oppressor.'

Apartheid

✑✏✑

Apartheid, 'living apart', became the policy of the national government of South Africa after two parties, the Reunited National Party and the Afrikaner Party, electioneering on the policy together, gained a narrow majority of five seats in 1948. Despite obtaining only 40% of the vote, they were able to win because of the weighting of white rural Afrikaans constituencies. The two parties merged and formed the National Party, which held sway then for nearly half a century.

Whilst there were significant historical antecedents for a discriminatory racial policy in Southern Africa (stretching back to the earliest times of European settlement), the rigorous intellectual and biblical bases for the policy, the extent and thoroughness of implementation, the ruthless use of force, and the manipulation of the law and the media taken together were new to South Africa. By 1948, there had been one contemporary international precedent, the rise and power of National Socialism, with its elitist, genetic Aryan policies in Germany; indeed there had been support in South Africa for the German Nazi Party during the Second World War. It is said that Afrikaners 'held that it was impossible, impracticable and ungodly for the different races and cultures to live as one', as reported in Wikipedia.

Over the next forty years South Africa was to experience a major social engineering initiative based on racist policies. Yet it is worth remembering some earlier examples of such discrimination. The earliest segregated township was developed by the government after the outbreak of bubonic plague in Cape Town in 1902, with several thousand Khoekhoe, Malay and mixed-race people being moved to Uitvlugt, on the edge of the Cape Flats, some 20 kilometres from the city centre. Then in 1913 the Land Act allocated 13% of the most infertile and marginal land in the country to tribal African reserves, to be home to an estimated 80% of the whole South African population. In 1923 the Native Urban Areas Act designated white urban areas and required African men in cities and towns to carry permits, which came to be known as passes. Anyone without a pass would be arrested and sent to a rural area. It is clear therefore that seeds for the later policy of apartheid were sown decades before the formation of the

National Party in 1948. Interestingly, however, to exclude natives from the Cape Colony, the first such pass was introduced in Cape Town by Earl Macartney as early as 1797.

Looking at the lives of ordinary folk in the non-white community in South Africa gives an insight into the effects that apartheid could have on a family. During our November 2011 visit to Cape Town we spent parts of two days with 'June', our guide and driver. June, with her family, had lived in District Six until 1974, when they were forced to leave. Her Irish father had come out to South Africa with his parents in 1947. Her mother in the apartheid classification was 'coloured Asian', as was June, yet her father and elder sister were classified as 'white'. Clearly the authorities saw the sister as having white ethnic attributes, whilst June had Asian attributes. This was to lead the sister to a privileged university education and a professional career, a way forward which had been impossible for June.

The marriage of June's parents was illegal and they even had to make sure that they did not go out together. June has the painful memory of her father and sister walking on one side of the street, and her mother and herself walking parallel on the other side, with her questioning her mother as to why they could not walk together. Another memory is of the police knocking on the door at night and her mother quickly putting on an apron to answer the door and pretending to be the maid. The reason for this came to her only in her teens when, for the first time, she saw in a document that she had been classified as coloured Asian, knowing as she did that her father and sister were classified as white. She said that there were few happy memories from her childhood, and that the best times were when the family were safely within the confines of their home.

We asked June how she and her family had felt on the release of Mandela in 1990. She said that they had been puzzled because they did not know who he was, nor what the ANC was, the censorship having been so tight. She had dreamed of freedom, but had never expected to see it. Mandela's presidency and the democracy in 1994 were a great release for everybody and warmly welcomed. She is very happy these days, free, employed and with a future to look forward to.

To understand and explain such a story, we must turn to the major apartheid policies of the National Party, which were enacted from 1949 onwards, and which affected this South African family of Irish and Asian descent, torn as it was between being 'white' and 'coloured Asian'.

The Prohibition of Mixed Marriages Act of 1949 prohibited marriage between persons of different races and the Immorality Act of 1950 made sexual relations with a person of a different race a criminal offence. Fundamental to the effort to implement this legislation was the Population Registration Act of 1950. This formalised racial classification and required all persons over the age of eighteen to carry an identity card specifying their racial group. Not only was there a classification into 'white', 'black', 'coloured' and 'Indian'; the latter two were divided into sub-classifications.

There were particular problems relating to the 'coloured' group, made up of people of mixed descent. Going back over the centuries the San, Khoi, Bantu, European, Indian and Malay peoples had intermingled. The temptation also was to try to use this category to cover others, for example Jews, Chinese and Japanese. This was to lead to political problems internationally and to some weird and pragmatic redefinitions. For example, immigrants from Japan, Taiwan and South Korea became honorary white people. Indian South Africans had perhaps the misfortune (or was it an opportunity?) of being classified as either Asian, Indian, black or coloured, but they were never white. South African Indonesians and Malays, known as Cape Malays, were classified as coloured, but Filipinos were 'black'.

There were many anomalies in the decision making and religion also could come into the equation. We met a man who had Scottish grandparents and a Scottish father, he had a Scottish name, but he had married a Muslim woman and had been classified as coloured; he said that this had happened because anybody who was a Muslim could not be classified as white.

The other major apartheid policy, the separation of races into different areas, was the Group Areas Act of 1950, in a sense a development of the above 1923 legislation and other acts including the Native Urban Areas Consolidation Act of 1945. The Group Areas Act provided for the designation of separate areas for, for example, white, black, coloured and Asian people, and later this became the basis for forcible removal, as happened to the family above in 1974 when they had to leave District Six. A 'group area' was to be for the exclusive ownership and occupation of one racial group and it was to be a criminal offence for a member of one racial group to live or own land in an area designated for another racial group.

Map 1 shows the notional division of broader Cape Town between the 'white', 'coloured' and 'black' peoples. Looking at the situation today, the paradoxes are clear. For example Langa Township, largely a Xhosa community, is in what was supposedly a coloured area and Ocean View,

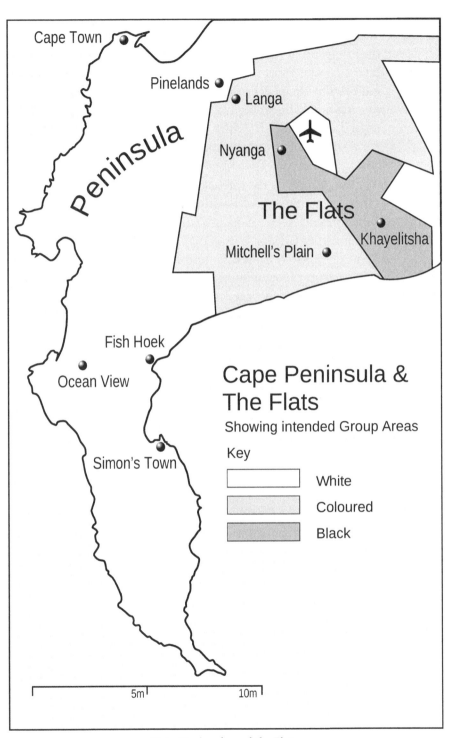

Cape Peninsula and the Flats

largely a coloured community, is in what was supposedly a white area. However, the intention of the Act was very clear: to allocate the peninsula and the western coastal areas to the white population and to consign the coloured and black people to the Flats.

The Prevention of Illegal Squatting Act of 1951 empowered the government to demolish black shanty towns, aimed at white group areas where such dwellings were unwelcome, and forced white employers to provide housing for any black workers they employed. In relation to the notion of separate 'homelands' for black people this policy was implemented further by the Bantu Authorities Act of 1951, the Promotion of Black Self-Government Act of 1959 and the Black Homeland Citizenship Act of 1970. It is estimated that between 1960 and 1983 3.5 million non-white people were removed from their homes.

The aim was to have independent black states within South Africa, self-governing and with their own citizens. Progressively Transkei, Bophuthatswana, Venda and Ciskei were declared to be independent and 8 million Africans lost their South African citizenship, legally becoming citizens of one of ten tribally based self-governing homelands called Bantustans. According to Martin Meredith, one government minister declared: 'If our policy is taken to its full logical conclusion as far as the black people are concerned, there will be not one black man with South African citizenship.' It is noteworthy that these 'homelands' were scattered through South Africa, and represented a small proportion of the nation's land, around 15%. They were overpopulated and were not economically viable. Meredith concludes:

> [T]he economic base supporting the homelands was pitifully inadequate ... there were few roads or railways, no major ports or cities, poor natural resources and land that was badly depleted by overpopulation and poor husbandry. They remained impoverished backwaters, inhabited by an impoverished peasantry and dependent on handouts from Pretoria and remittances from migrant labour.

This labour force provided white employers with cheap and transient workers, the migrants being separated from their families and living in shanty towns, often in male hostels or having very long daily travel to work.

Another special feature of the social engineering was the drive to eliminate settlements known as 'black spots', which were fragments of land occupied by non-white people, both black and coloured, within or right up against white designated areas. From the 1960s onwards non-white people were uprooted from these areas, whole communities being moved, by force where necessary, to areas which were unsuitable. Father Cosmas Desmond travelled across South Africa in 1969 and it is little surprise that he found a 'labyrinth of broken communities, broken families and broken lives'.

The major initiatives were reinforced by what has been described as 'petty apartheid', an odd epithet for measures which seem obscene and deeply divisive to outside observers. The Reservation of Separate Amenities Act of 1951 intended separate benches, beaches, buses and, particularly important, separate hospitals, schools and universities for the different races. Illustrative of the socially divisive nature of this was the proliferation of 'whites only' signboards in public areas.

In support of the apartheid policy, legislated by a government based on 'fancy franchise' whereby from 1970 onwards only white people had the vote, a hugely disproportionate part of the public purse was spent on employment measures and social infrastructure supporting the white population.

Petty apartheid

Overall between 1948 and 1988 there were 165 pieces of 'apartheid legislation'. During apartheid the white minority, around 15% of the population, controlled South Africa, and this was made possible through the limited franchise. The fact that a series of disenfranchisement moves were unconstitutional was negated by the government as it overrode entrenched clauses of the Constitution. The best example was the 1952 High Court of Parliament Bill, which gave Parliament the power to overrule court decisions.

Later, through raising the number of judges on the Appeal Court, and the expedient of a temporary doubling of the size of the Senate, a joint session of Parliament passed the Separate Representation of Voters Act of 1956, which transferred coloured voters from the common voters roll in the Cape to a new coloured voters roll. They could now vote for four white representatives, but even this right was withdrawn in 1969. A Supreme Court appeal in 1956 failed in the court packed with pro-National Party judges.

The notion that black people did have the vote and self-determination, but only in their homelands, was completely unacceptable to the black people themselves, and other disenfranchisement measures affecting the rest of the non-white population had a similar impact on those racial groups. By the 1980s these chickens began to come home to roost as pressure for the vote grew from all the disenfranchised groups, with the growing realisation that the only viable way to combat the system was to gain political power.

As both external and internal pressure developed the Botha government in 1980 decided to extend the franchise to the coloured and Indian groups by establishing their right to elect their own representatives to two new chambers and thereby to govern their own areas. This was another form of racial discrimination and excluded the black population, who were seen to have self-governing rights in their own homelands but not to be citizens of South Africa. The initiative was widely opposed and in 1983 a coalition of 300 organisations established the United Democratic Front (UDF) to oppose the proposed constitutional changes. Support arose from churches, trade unions, student bodies and community organisations. The coalition cut across lines of class, colour, religion and politics and demanded a united and democratic South Africa, universal franchise and the abolishment of all of the apartheid policies. Nevertheless, elections were held for the new tricameral parliament and the associated constitutional set-up in August 1984. The turnout was low, however, and very serious outbreaks of violence began in September, which were to continue into the early nineties.

In addition to the narrow franchise, a key instrument to establish the apartheid system was educational policy. The attitude to the idea of educational opportunity for all is best expressed by a statement by Dr Verwoerd (Minister for Native Affairs 1950–1958 and Prime Minister 1958–1966), quoted by Levine:

> When I have control of Native education I will reform it so that the natives will be taught from childhood to realise that equality with the Europeans is not for them ... What is the use of teaching a Bantu child mathematics when it cannot use it in practice? ... Education must train and teach people in accordance with their opportunities in life.

This sort of thinking from the top of national government influenced educational policy and investment. Meredith writes that in the early 1970s 'sixteen times more was spent on white education per pupil than on black education'. The results for the non-white people were inferior, over-crowded school buildings, both understaffed and inadequately equipped. Only 5% of African pupils went into the secondary schools, from which there was also a drop-out. On leaving school there were relatively few employment opportunities and these were largely in the unskilled jobs: not surprising, given the policy elaborated by Verwoerd. This was to build up huge pressures against the government in the 1970s and 1980s.

The key instruments in the apartheid era were political power (based on limited franchise, legislation and the skewing of the judiciary to enable the Constitution to be outflanked), an elitist and racist educational system, and a vast bureaucracy. None of this would have worked, however, without the repressive security system, which included the State Security Council, the police, the armed services and a network of informers. This became even more repressive when Botha became Prime Minister amidst pending disaster for South African policies at the frontiers and within the neighbouring Angola, Mozambique and Rhodesia, coupled with sporadic barely controllable violence at home and the emergence of active community associations and trade unions, the bans on which had been lifted to try to lessen the growing head of steam. Botha sent troops and paramilitary police into the townships, and police death squads were unleashed. To quote from Meredith: 'A secret police counter insurgency unit set up in 1980 ... soon was involved in

Mandela's last step to freedom

bombing, arson, kidnapping and assassination.' Nevertheless, or maybe partly because of this, the black consciousness movement, followed by a resurgent ANC and strong student unrest and the work of the UDF, built up further pressure and violence increased.

In stages the answer, centring on the release of Nelson Mandela and co-operation to find jointly a peaceful solution, emerged early in the 90s and finally there were elections in 1994 under a universal franchise. This photo represents Nelson Mandela taking the last step on his long journey to freedom as he leaves the Victor Verster Prison, now the Groot Drakenstein Prison, in 1990. His raised right fist is the symbol of his mission of 'power for the people', 'amandla awethu' in isiZulu.

Observers and historians have considered and weighed the various influences on the destruction of the system of apartheid. There has been much stress on international change, especially the effects of the ending of the Cold War on the policy repositioning of the USA and UK. The demise of Soviet communism, the ending of South African military involvement around its northern borders, and the need to accept otherwise unpalatable regimes in Angola, Mozambique and Namibia also were factors. The flight of international investment and the heavy expenses of security and the military had combined to critically reduce the nation's gold and currency reserves. The vulnerability is demonstrated by the fact that in 1985, with the ending of USA and UK investment in South Africa, the rand dropped 35% in value. There seemed to be no way to reduce the upsurge of violence and discontent.

What is certain is that the mood of the white population was changing significantly. Parents had been losing their children in warfare; returning troops, some maimed, were disillusioned with what the fighting had been about. In universities and colleges many young

Afrikaners were looking at things in a different way. Afrikaner intellectuals, both secular and religious, were questioning the philosophical basis for apartheid and noting the detrimental effects of the system. In the white Dutch churches there had been a major change in theological thinking, which was influencing the laity, and many other faith groups were continuing to be influential. White South Africans were seeing their nation to be an international pariah, isolated in sport and religion, pilloried in the United Nations and other international fora and therefore facing harmful sanctions. To cap it all, businesses were suffering because of the labour restrictions, the shortage of skilled labour and the economic uncertainty arising from continuing violence.

The key decisions, to share power, even to risk losing power, could only be made by people, the very people who were in power in the national government, and they now knew they could sustain neither apartheid nor the disenfranchised basis for the existence of apartheid. It was fortunate that, in the face of all of these pressures, there was a powerful, politically sensitive and pragmatic person leading South Africa in the early 1990s, President de Klerk. The scene was set therefore for a completely new story to start in 1994 with President Mandela, the unification government and the 'rainbow nation'.

In the light of this story it was a remarkable privilege for me to be at Grosvenor House in London on 25 January 2016 on the occasion of the ubuntu.london presentation of 'Life Is Wonderful!' in support of Global Citizen, the great international charity working to alleviate extreme poverty. This evening involved the celebration of 'three genuine icons of the anti-apartheid movement', Denis Goldberg, Ahmed 'Kathy' Kathrada and Andrew Mlangeni, the first two of whom were there for the evening and able to share their experience with us. The three of them, accused along with Nelson Mandela, were known respectively as no. 3, no. 5 and no. 10 in the 1963/64 Rivonia Trial, and between them had spent seventy-four years in prison.

We heard many things that evening and it was a time of reflection, joy and some tears. What I came away with particularly was the story of Bram Fischer QC, who led the defence team and saved the lives of Mandela and the ANC leadership. Of all the Rivonia defendants and their lawyers he was the only one who did not live to see a free and democratic South Africa. He died in prison in 1975 following his own sentence to life imprisonment for treason and the especially harsh treatment he received in jail. Of Bram Fischer Mandela wrote:

As an Afrikaner whose conscience forced him to reject his own heritage and be ostracised by his own people, he showed a level of courage and sacrifice that was in a class by itself ... Bram was a free man who fought against his own people to ensure the freedom of others.

Explaining the name of this 'Life Is Wonderful!' event: when the sentence was read out at the end of the Rivonia Trial, the judge spoke so quietly that those in the galleries could not hear. The mother of Denis Goldberg, expecting the death penalty for her son, shouted that she hadn't heard the sentence, to which Denis shouted back, 'It's life – life is wonderful!' So it turned out to be, because Mandela and the ANC leadership did not go to the gallows and were available to lead South Africa between 1990 and 1994 to freedom and democracy without the anticipated nation-wide bloodbath.

District Six Forced Removals

~~~

Driving from the Waterfront in Cape Town you can join the N2 at a major roundabout junction and drive northwards to join the M3 road, signposted to Muizenburg. The M3 skirts Table Mountain, which towers above it, and the road is elevated above the city and the start of the Cape Flats. This can be a hairy drive in the rush hour, but otherwise, taking one's time, the occasional glance to the side reveals fascinating scenes of city to the left and of rugged mountainside to the right.

Looking downwards to the south of the city centre, we see an extensive area of what seems to be a grassy wasteland along the flank of Table Mountain. Oddly scattered across the wasteland are churches and mosques, each isolated from the other. As reported by Cape Town History and Heritage, this is 'one of the most tangible and evocative testimonies' to the apartheid period.

This area was known as District Six, and has been renamed Zonnebloem, the name of the original farm in that area. It is a devastating monument to the ruthlessness of the national government in implementing its apartheid policies, after the election victory of the National Party in 1948, which was narrowly won on an apartheid manifesto.

'Apartheid', translated from the Afrikaans, means 'the state of being apart', and the key legislation to apartheid policies included the Group Areas Act of 1950. An acidic commentary about this and other policies was in the *Torch*, 3 October 1962, one of the newspapers displayed in the District Six Museum, under the headlines 'Tribalstans' and 'Government Plans to Buy Safety':

> The government is proudly boasting that it is prepared to spend vast sums of money to buy a longer lease of life for the pattern of Herrenvolk oppression and super exploitation it is imposing on the rightless millions of the land. At the same time it is clearly realised that money alone cannot buy Herrenvolk immortality and a constant struggle against hostility at home and abroad has to be waged.

District Six was given its name in 1867, when it became known as the Sixth Municipal District of Cape Town. A built-up area of about 1.5

square kilometres, it had developed from the 1830s onwards just off the centre of Cape Town to the west of Company Gardens and to the south of the castle, with close links with both the city and the port. Early on it was a community of freed slaves, artisans and labourers, merchants and immigrants. There is commentary that initially the area consisted of small houses, run by slum landlords, along narrow lanes without water or sewerage. Some houses had only one room, with a toilet in the back yard, and housed as many as sixteen people, as reported by Cape Town History and Heritage.

Resettlement had an early precedent, as thousands of black people were forcibly resettled in 1901, when 2,000 houses were demolished and rebuilt. Description later is of an overcrowded but vibrant community of workers and artisans and small businesses, with people well located for work in the nearby docks, factories and city centre. Noor Ebrahim, in his book *Noor's Story: My Life in District Six*, writes that the district:

> ... was originally a mixed community of freed slaves, immigrants, labourers, merchants and artisans. Later it included a different kind of mix – artists, politicians, businessmen, musicians, writers, teachers, sheiks, priests, gangsters, sportsmen, housewives and always lots of children ... Sixty to seventy thousand people lived together in great harmony until disaster struck our community.

Others still commented on crowded and unhealthy conditions, exploitative landlords and crime, and there were moves in the 1930s and 1940s to try to improve the area. Cape Town Heritage states that '"control" had become a feature of urban planning and clearly shows how the spatial concepts prevalent in town planning at that time fitted neatly with the political ideology'. Whatever the case, on 11 February 1966, District Six was designated as an area to be occupied only by white people as defined in the Population Registration Act.

The disaster stemmed from the implementation of the 1950 Group Areas Act, which with various changes was operative until it and the related laws succeeding it were repealed in June 1991 by the Abolition of Racially Based Land Measures Act. The 1950 Act was based on, and drew together, several strands of racially discriminatory legislation certainly tracing back to the start of the twentieth century, but with ethnic roots deep in the attitudes and practices of the nineteenth century and even earlier. Moreover, the initiative had been foreshadowed in the 1930s by town planning and by the publication of the first municipality redevelopment plan in 1940. Such thinking paved the way for the social engineering to be so brilliantly codified and ruthlessly executed during the apartheid era.

The Act of 1950 required that urban areas be racially segregated. A group area was designated for the exclusive ownership and occupation of one racial group and it would be a criminal offence for a member of one racial group to live in or own land in an area set aside for another race. This Act, and later supporting legislation, laid the foundations for what was to happen to District Six in the years to come when, in 1966, it was declared to be a 'white group area'. As concluded by Professor Alan Mabin of Pretoria University, in addition to the notion of segregation of black people, the Group Areas Act:

> 'at least potentially extended compulsory general segregation to "Coloureds"; centralised control over racial segregation, effectively undermining municipal autonomy; laid the basis for long-range, wide-scale land allocation planning; provided for retroactive segregation; and massively interfered with concepts of property rights generally.'

What was to happen was made possible by a large and efficient bureaucracy, a powerful internal security system and the determination of the national government to separate the different races of South Africa into defined areas. Enabling legislation included the various pass laws, the prohibition of mixed marriages (1949), and population registration (1950).

Whilst all of this legislation in the apartheid era was driven by Afrikaner philosophy, it is only fair to record that the thinking traces back to colonial times and notions of racial superiority arising from white groups of various nationalities, and it was not completely unacceptable to some of the English-speaking white South Africans. Indeed the first resettlement from District Six was in 1901, when black people were transferred away, supposedly because of an outbreak of bubonic plague in the centre of Cape Town.

Decades later, following the 11 February 1966 declaration of its 'white group area' status, it took nearly ten years to clear most of District Six, to change it from a teeming inner city suburb to a 'dust bowl', retaining a number of scattered faith centres, largely Christian but including mosques, as the law did not permit the closure of religious centres.

It seems extraordinary that the government did not clear the area completely and that there has been so little development since the 1970s. It is understood, however, that such was the local, national and international uproar about this initiative, including a 'Hands Off District Six' campaign, that protest bodies were able to dissuade developers and potential residents 'by ensuring that the area was considered to be tainted'. Some 60,000 people were removed, two thirds to the Cape Flats, including Mitchell's Plain. In the 1980s, frustrated by the lack of private development, the government occupied part of the area with housing for police and army personnel and erected the Cape Technical College.

The 1994 democratic election, however, was followed by new policies for the area. Families able to show that they had been removed from District Six were invited to register for resettlement there, or for financial compensation. There has been some development close to two mosques at the eastern end, but extensive swathes of grassland cover the foundations of much of the bulldozed settlement. It is understood that of the many claims registered, only 194 houses have been built, and the perception of my taxi driver is that many claimants prefer financial compensation to the chance to go back. When I met Noor Ebrahim again

Wasteland with churches

in October 2015, he expressed great frustration that twenty years had passed and there had been little restitution to date.

It is relevant to recap on the Noor Ebrahim story, which is about his grandparents, his parents and his own generation in District Six. It is a case study. A man from Surat near Bombay arrives in District Six over a century ago. He marries Fanny Grainger, a Scottish girl, and they have nine sons and two daughters. But she dies in 1922 in Mecca. He then marries Mariam, who bears four sons and five daughters, but she dies in 1939. Two more marriages yield three more children. This man, Noor's grandfather, is a highly successful businessman and a religious leader. Such a life is the basis for a burgeoning family within and spilling out from District Six.

Noor Eprahim is born in 1944. His story of growing up to adulthood reflects the sorts of memories that many of us have from all parts of the world: memories of home, parents, siblings, schooling, of eating and of playing the same games, from marbles to bok bok ('break the camel's back' in my British playground experience!) to football and cricket and rugby; memories of the shops, the cinema, and of the special occasions, of faith, of marriage and death, and fights and burglary. We have a sense of people at work and play, of the power of the extended family, of neighbourliness, of the living together of people of different colours and faiths. This is a whimsical story made more whimsical by the reader's knowledge that this seething social unit was being edged to extinction, that for tens of thousands of people nothing would be the same again from the late 1960s onwards.

The method of the clearance, an evil which Noor Ebrahim describes in his book, was to warn residents street by street, giving, say, a month's notice. This story closes, therefore, with the thought that on designated days bulldozers would demolish houses and shops. One newspaper, displayed in the District Six Museum, reported as follows:

> Bulldozers and wrecking crews are tearing the heart out of District Six … and they are tearing the heart out of the people that have lived there for generations. To outsiders it is a festering slum, but to them it is home, a home that will soon be gone, as they are moved to the Cape Flats. But they don't want those *nice little houses*. They want District Six.

Simon's Town Forced Removals

The first part of this story draws on a booklet produced by the Simon's Town Historical Society, 'Simon's Town and the Forced Removals of the 1960s', and displays in the Simon's Town Museum have also been very helpful.

The relatively recent history of Simon's Town records the forced removal of black and coloured people in the late 1960s. The town was proclaimed to be a white group area on 1 September 1967, this having been first proposed in 1959.

It is wrong to conclude that the whole white population in South Africa supported the rigid apartheid policies and that there were no antis amongst the Afrikaans-speaking population, or, indeed, that there were no supporters of the apartheid policies amongst the English-speaking white population. Proof for us of the opposition to the policies came in February 2014 when we visited Simon's Town again and spotted an intriguing memorial near the Jubilee Garden, which stated:

> To the memory of generations of our fellow citizens
> who dwelt here in peace and harmony until removed
> by edict of 1967
>
> *Erected by their fellow citizens*

Indeed it is very significant that at the boards of enquiry in 1959 and 1965, which were held to gauge the feelings of the local community, not one person in Simon's Town was found to be in favour of forced removals.

Concerning the memorial, and the families who were forced to leave Simon's Town, a secretary of the Simon's Town Historical Society, Audrey Reid, has written as follows:

It is a moving little memorial. Each year on 24th September or the nearest Saturday many of them come to the Museum, have a look at the Simon's Town Room and renew old acquaintances and then march up the main street to the Memorial where they say a few prayers and lay a wreath. If the weather is bad they meet in the Town Hall, which is just past the Square. They usually bring a grandchild, which is good.

There was an enormous local reaction from the white community, including petitions from the Member of Parliament and from the Mayor and Council against the whole resettlement initiative. Indeed there was very significant opposition from a number of local bodies, including the Non-European Group Areas Organising Committee, Members of the South African Navy in Simon's Town, the Chamber of Commerce, the Town Municipality, the Glencairn Civic Association, the Indian Association, the Roman Catholic Church, the Methodist Church, the Anglican Church, the Mosque Trustees and the Black Sash. All of the submissions were unsuccessful.

It is said that the black people were given a weekend to move, being dispersed to Langa, Gugulethu and Nyanga. The coloured people are said to have been given more time, up to a year, and indeed house owners could let their houses to 'qualified' persons, presumably white. They were moved to Ocean View, Retreat, Heathfield and Grassy Park. The Ocean View case is interesting, because about half of the coloured residents were sent there. The Simon's Town municipality sent lorries to help them get their furniture to that area, although this piece of information is at odds with a statement that people had to finance their own removal – perhaps some groups did and other groups did not!

The hiatus and the local anguish are well captured by extracts of the letter to the *Cape Argus* written in 1968 by Mr HC Willis (Dumps) a former deputy mayor of Simon's Town, whose wife, Barbara, was a leader in the Black Sash movement.

> Sir, – Simon's Town is dead – murdered by the Group Areas Act. It will of course continue as a collection of buildings in which people work, but the spirit of the place is departed.
>
> Already, the cheerful, happy, peaceful, friendly atmosphere, which so much impressed newcomers and visitors, is no more: a pall of gloom has taken its place.
>
> Nor will it ever return, as it was a result of two and a half centuries of peaceful relations between persons of all colours and races arising from the respectful appreciation of each other's good points and a kindly tolerance of their failures.
>
> A living entity has been destroyed. What have those who perpetrated the destruction put in its place? Nothing – a blank, a town without a soul.

Within three years the population of the town had fallen by a half. Empty buildings and streets were left forlorn to the elements, falling into disrepair and finally being demolished to make way for redevelopment, which has continued over the decades. The photo shows part of the abandoned 'Big House' in Waterfall Road, around 1975, which had been the home of the Adams and Andrews families, and which was demolished in 1976.

Abandoned house

Many of the new or renovated houses now are too expensive for those families which had left, and indeed too expensive for the children and grandchildren of remaining long-standing residents. Confirming this, the secretary of the Historical Society has stated that over the last twenty years no black people and very few coloured people have returned to Simon's Town. This is hardly surprising because the buildings that they had occupied over many decades, empty and becoming ramshackle, were demolished and made way later for much more expensive redevelopment. Quoting from the Historical Association booklet:

Most of the original homes were made of adobe bricks and were one hundred years old, they fell into disrepair and were razed after twenty years. Some of the land in the Upper Mt. Pleasant area went to the navy and the middle of the town was redeveloped ... for schooling and local government.

Effectively an integrated economy in which people had jobs and a place and a life within their own community was transformed; neither that life, nor their homes, nor their jobs existed in the way that they did prior to 1967.

On the day of our visit in February 2014 we crossed over the road from the Jubilee Garden memorial to buy a straw hat for Pam, as the scorching sun was beating down on us. We got talking to an elderly Indian gentleman, who clearly owned the shop. We mentioned the memorial to him and he said that it had been a terrible time. In stages the non-white population were being removed, first the black and then the coloured people. It was to be the turn of the Indians next, but for some unknown reason this never happened. Later, elsewhere, we enquired about why Indians had not been resettled and received two answers. One was to the effect that the authorities did not know where to move the Indians to. The second was particularly intriguing – to quote: 'if the Indians had left us we would have had no shops'. In the event, some of the Indian families moved away of their own volition and many now live in the Rylands area, a suburb to the east of Cape Town and directly to the south of Langa Township, which is largely a Xhosa community.

The 'forced removals' changed the racial structure of the town greatly, as shown in the table below:

Table 1: Racial makeup of Simon's Town

CENSUS	WHITE	%	COLOURED	%	BLACK	%	INDIAN/ ASIAN	%	TOTAL
1960	1482	22	3579	54	1500	22	115	2	6676
1975	3130	90	80	2.3	110	3	167	4.7	3487

Towards the end of March in 2014, in revisiting the town, we called in on the Amlay Museum and talked to Mr Davidson, who, through his Muslim wife, had connections in Simon's Town going back several generations. Of a Scottish background, he had become a Muslim when he married Patti Amlay and for this reason had been classified, with his wife, as coloured.

His family had been moved from the very house the museum is now in, a building the top floor of which he and his wife now had reoccupied. It was a paradox that this beautiful building, on the seashore before recent developments of the naval base, had been owned by the family, and now they had been able to return to it as long as they paid rent to the new owners, the South African Navy.

On the ground floor the museum has a large and fascinating range of exhibits, including many photographs illustrating the lives of the wider Asian and Muslim community and signs of racial harmony and integration. Now Mr Davidson says that since the resettlement 'many of the coloured people are starving in the townships', which I gather to some is a contentious and somewhat apocalyptic view.

In October 2015, revisiting Simon's Town to review this story, I again visited the very interesting museum. On a notice board outside was a declaration from the Office of the Land Claims Commissioner of Western Cape that the Office 'urgently needs to locate the following Simon's Town claimants in connection with their land claims'. There were forty-seven family names, against each of which was an address or area in Simon's Town, the subject of a possible claim, and the current address, if known, of the family. For several of the names no current address was shown, but nearly half of the families now had addresses in the townships of Ocean View and Grassy Plain to which they had been removed nearly half a century earlier.

Two decades after the end of apartheid, but viewed by many to be too little and too late, some restitution is being made. For example, as quoted in the July 2015 Bulletin of the Simon's Town Historical Society, reproducing a newspaper article:

> On Thursday 23 April Mayor Patricia de Lille handed title deeds of a plot in Cotton Road, Simon's Town, to Mr Abduragman Aziz of Retreat. The Aziz family owned several plots in Simon's Town, until they removed in 1971 in terms of the Group Areas Act ... In 1995 the family started the long process of lodging a restitution claim through the Lands Claims Commission ... The plot, valued at Rand 1.1 million, was handed over to the Aziz family at no cost.
>
> *Michelle Saffer*, False Bay Echo, *30 April 2015*

It is therefore appropriate to end this story as follows. On 9 November 2015 I was taken by the coloured Kenny family to look around part of the Ocean View neighbourhood. I went into two apartment blocks, which people had been moved to in 1972, and also into a new house in the adjacent new City of Cape Town development for the less well-off. This sort of development of rented social accommodation, with a combined lounge/kitchen and two bedrooms, seems to be the standard, with mains sewerage, electricity and piped water. It is greatly prized as a way of moving from both apartment block and shanty accommodation, so let me take you back to one of the apartments.

I climb up very steep stairs to the third floor and am introduced to Enid and her husband. She is the great-grandmother who lives in two bedrooms and a kitchen with nine others; sometimes it has been up to fifteen, making up four generations of her family. The apartment is very congested with furniture, poorly decorated and a distressing sight. She has been in it for forty-three years, but in no way does she want to go to better accommodation nearby, as this is now her home.

Coloured people, she and her family were removed forty-three years ago from their home near Simon's Town, where, using local timber and spring water, they had established a farm growing vegetables and fruit for themselves and the local market. They had been happy and self-sufficient, but they had been in an area designated 'white'. Their story is that of coloured farmers and also of coloured farm labourers and their families being arbitrarily removed through the group areas policy. Their land became the property of the City of Cape Town, the farms falling into disuse, and the self-sufficient farmsteads supplying local communities disappearing. This was evidenced clearly, but without explanation, during a Simon's Town Historical Society lecture on the history of the nearby Silvermine Valley, which I attended on 28 October 2015, the comment being that all the farms had disappeared.

Later, on 9 November, the Kenny family, who had kindly been guiding me as I drove around, showed me the mountainside where Nadia Petersen's father had been a farm worker before these removals. Now the site has been sold to a developer by the City of Cape Town and is being cleared for a new, very upmarket housing estate.

Of what has happened to Enid's family, Nadia Petersen wrote to me on my return to England, and I quote selectively but verbatim from her commentary:

Enid was relocated 43 years ago to a City of Cape Town rented three room flat in Larkspur Court, Ocean View. Over the years, sometimes up to fifteen people lived there in dire conditions (currently there are nine); forced removals have placed her in a position . . . where she could never find a way of providing for herself and her family, with no education the process of having a better life was one she could never achieve. Then you can easily say that forced removals have impacted her life – as a child she lost everything, in her mind trucks just came and they had to load whatever they could and what was left behind they could never go back to where they lived again for it – now she lives as a hoarder, furniture and boxes and boxes of clutter. She only walks to her balcony and window, she baths and cooks in her bedroom, her kitchen is partly divided a bedroom for her son, in the second bedroom all the grandchildren sleep – a little girl who lost everything has created a need of clutter and safety around her to a state of where her children, their children, their girlfriends and boyfriends with their own children stay, many of whom are unemployed, out of school, using drugs and on government welfare – it is a state of psychological, emotional and mental problems that is the worst impact forced removals had on a family who could never pass on a form of uplifting to themselves and their generation.

Enid's apartment block

Enid is only one of many similar cases in Ocean View where the work of social empowering and uplifting is a cry out in a country where the prospect of applying for jobs is poor and where parents do not have money to give their children a good education or even study further and if they do succeed they always face the challenge of being in a government system where the percentage of jobs available for coloureds are the last. Work is allocated on a quota system by race: Africans, whites, Asians and coloureds. Many would say we are living in Apartheid reversed where the Africans are in control, the whites second and the coloureds still last yet we also went through the process of Apartheid, forced removal and fighting for freedom.

Nadia contributes again to this book, through the final part of the epilogue.

Faith Groups and Apartheid

cㄝ⁊ᴄ⌒ᴐ

Our first church service ever in South Africa was in St George's Cathedral, Cape Town, at the All Saints' Day Mass on 6 November 2011. This was a very moving occasion for a couple who had followed the fortunes of South Africa from university days, over fifty years earlier. We were part of the perhaps unhelpful group of people involved in sanctions, for us the end of the best quality but cheap 'sherry' that we had been enjoying in Cambridge in the late 1950s. We had watched apartheid from 6,000 miles away and agreed with sanctions, barely understanding what was going on, but as Anglicans sympathising with people such as Bishop Trevor Huddleston and the Venerable Joost de Blank as they faced the consequences of their stand against apartheid.

Now in 2011 we were seated with a multi-ethnic congregation, worshipping in English, Afrikaans and Xhosa, with a church leadership and choir reflecting the rainbow nation. The service sheet was in the three languages, as were the intercessions. We even had immediately behind us a lady with a penetrating voice who sang the hymns, verse by verse, successively in English, Afrikaans and Xhosa, thereby making a special point. The Reverend Frank English was the preacher; his theme was sainthood historically, but now seeing the need for the saintliness of thoughtful reticence, in a world dominated by the immediacy of ready answers. We all took communion together and everything felt right.

The following Sunday, Remembrance Sunday, we were in St Mary's on the Braak in Stellenbosch. Again a multi-ethnic congregation and the three languages were the features and we felt united across race in coming to God through the Anglican community. The rector in his sermon spoke about interdependence. He used as an analogy Chief Rabbi Gren's test with his congregation to show the significance of a black spot on a piece of white paper. The white paper is nothing, completely blank, but it is brought to life by the black spot in the middle of it, and yet the black spot exists against the essential white background. The culmination of the service was very moving, as the rector read out Siegfried Sassoon's First World War poem 'Soldier Boy', which we listened to seated next to the memorial for a young trooper, raised by his comrades during the First World War.

Later that morning, on going back to our lodgings opposite the main Dutch Reform Church, we saw several hundreds of the congregation leaving, all white except for half a dozen black girls who turned out to be a visiting choir. In our ignorance, we were startled by this sight and puzzled by this Stellenbosch experience. An explanation follows, many of the facts relying on a 1985 paper by JA Loader: a South African university academic with wide international experience, a writer and a minister of the Nederduitsch Hervormde Kerk.

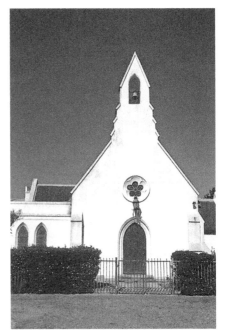

St Mary's on the Braak

The census featuring a survey of church membership in 1980 in South Africa indicated that 77% of the population called themselves Christians. The biggest group were the black independent churches, some 2,000 covering 5 million people. Second was the Roman Catholic Church with 2.35 million, third was the Methodist with 2.11 million, and fifth was the Anglican group with 1.61 million. Fourth was the Nederduitse Gereformeerde Kerk or NGK (for white people) with 1.69 million, sixth was the NG Church in Africa (for black people) and eighth was the NG Mission Church (for coloured people). Together, the three NG churches had a membership of 3.47 million. Moreover, two other Afrikaner churches, for white people only, together had a membership of around 440,000. Other Protestant churches together seemed to have a combined membership of 2.6 million.

The organisation of the NGK into three racial groups explains what we were so surprised to see in Stellenbosch. We had moved during one morning from a multi-racial Anglican service in Stellenbosch, perhaps attended by a couple of hundred people, to witness just up the road several hundred people leaving an all-white service.

Looking back, the Churches Native Laws Amendment Act of 1957 had prohibited black people from attending white churches. It is said, however, that the act was never rigidly enforced and churches were one of the few places where races could mix. Ironically, the NGK, with its tripartite colour-based churches, *de facto* did not seem to need the law.

The question arises as to what the role of faith groups was in the setting up, development and ending of apartheid. We shall see that different Christian groups had differing influences and responses, that a group's policy might change with time, that the leadership of a group did not necessarily represent the view of congregations and that the roles of other faith groups need to be considered.

The 1985 analysis of JA Loader related to apartheid from its official inception to the response of various faith groups to the national government's major policy initiatives in the early 1980s. The analysis is significantly instructive and is a basis for some final conclusions here. Three groups of churches are classified in the political situation relating to apartheid: passive participants, the churches strongly critical, and the supportive churches.

Loader sees the passive participants as concentrating on the spiritual and avoiding the political debates in the 'ecclesiastical circles'. Within the passive group were the black independent churches, which had no or little interest in combating apartheid; indeed they might be seen as agents of acquiescence. 'They have assumed the role of helping their adherents to cope with the *status quo*, not of changing it,' writes Loader, suggesting this is a sort of Marxist opiate for the people. The Pentecostal churches, including the Apostolic Faith Mission and the Full Gospel Church, were seen to be another part of the passive group. There were also the conservative evangelical churches, including the Church of the Nazarene, the Baptists, Free Methodists and Free Lutherans, and the Anglican evangelical wing. A fourth passive category was seen to be the charismatic movement, centring on religious experience rather than current and political affairs.

Langa Gospel Church

Such a wide range of churches, some small and local, but together with the support of several million people, showed a tacit and sometimes explicit tendency to support the powers that be. More serious, however, was their alienation from the South African Council of Churches, and there was even loud criticism of that council by the conservative evangelicals, which damagingly received media attention.

The churches seemingly in opposition to apartheid had 7 million members and in their criticism of apartheid they were supported by the Roman Catholic Church with a membership of 2 million. The leaderships of the Protestant churches, especially through the South African Council of Churches (SACC), were in constant opposition to the National Party, although Loader questions whether the congregations of these churches were wholly united in supporting their leaderships all the time. The members of the SACC are the Methodist, Anglican, Presbyterian and Congregational churches, together the English-speaking churches but including all racial groups, and also the NG Church in Africa, the Mission Church and the Reformed Church in Africa, these last generally being black and coloured and Afrikaans-speaking.

The Afrikaans-speaking NG churches naturally were at odds with each other, given the separation into white, black and coloured churches. Such a separation traced back to the 1857 decision by the synod of the Cape Church which enabled separate NG churches for the different races, the decision arising from the fact that some white people did not want to share the communion table with non-white people. Much water passed under the bridge thereafter, leading to the deeply established tripartite separation of the NGK. It is ironic, therefore, that in 1978 in Ottawa at a meeting of the World Alliance of Reformed Churches some delegates from the 'black' reformed churches refused to take communion with delegates from the 'apartheid churches', the latter then being suspended from the Alliance.

It is worth noting, however, that similar questions about separate churches for the races had been raised within the Anglican Church in the nineteenth century, in relation to the mission churches and their representation on the diocesan synod. It took several decades to resolve this question, but it was more a reflection of apathy and paternalism than notions of racial separation before God, in the view of Mandy Goedhals in *Bounty in Bondage*. Moreover, whilst there is a significant record of Anglican churchmen protesting against apartheid (Archbishop Joost de Blank, Father Michael Scott, Father Trevor Huddleston, Bishop David

Russell, Archbishop Desmond Tutu, Bishop Sigisbert Ndwandwe, Father Geoffrey Moselane and Bishop James Kauluma), the point was made by the Revd Frank England that overall the anti movement consisted of protests, generally written, but not sustained resistance.

A wider perspective arises from Nelson Mandela, who very much appreciated the opposition to apartheid arising from faith groups other than the churches mentioned above. In 1997, at the Oxford Centre for Islamic Studies, he stated: 'The strength of inter-religious solidarity in action against apartheid, rather than mere harmony in co-existence, was critical in bringing that evil system down.' In 1991 he had addressed Hindus at their Diwali celebration in Durban, in 1992 the Free Ethiopian Church, in 1992 the Zionist Christians, in 1997 the 37th Congress of the Jewish Board of Deputies in Johannesburg and in 1998 the Muslim community in Johannesburg. Each address contained his gratitude for the contribution made by faith groups to education and health care for the black peoples, and his gratitude to the individuals within those faith groups who inspired and bravely led opposition to racism and to the apartheid system.

Critical to apartheid, in the decades of its genesis before 1948 and for the next forty years, was the intellectual and theological support of the white Dutch Reform Church (NGK), from which two apartheid period Prime Ministers were drawn (Strijdom and Verwoerd), hence the perceptive comment by Nelson Mandela in his address at Stellenbosch University, the leading intellectual home of Afrikaner nationalism, in October 1996:

> Last week saw an event of the greatest significance that originated right here in Stellenbosch ... the Stellenbosch Presbytery of the Dutch Reformed Church confessed before the Truth and Reconciliation Commission a collective share in the systemic injustice of our past. Neither the message this conveyed, nor the impact this will make on the process of reconciliation, is to be underestimated.

It is fitting that the Mandela Gold Plant is in the University of Stellenbosch Botanical Gardens, very near this major NG church.

Loader saw the three white Afrikaans churches as providing the government with a religious legitimacy for its policies, a legitimacy based on biblical texts, for example from Genesis, Deuteronomy, and the books of Ezra and Nehemiah. A reflection of how a Christian Afrikaner might view his or her place in the firmament can be taken from a statement by

Prime Minister DF Malan in 1938, on the centenary of the Battle of Blood River, quoted in Battle:

> The Trekkers received their task from God's hand. They gave their answer. They made their sacrifices. There is still a white race ... Separate development under the leadership of God's chosen instrument – the Afrikaner people – was the divine plan of South Africa.

Mandela Gold Plant

So after a quarter of a century of experiencing the practical and philosophical implications of apartheid, as late as 1974 the synod of the NGK still accepted separate development of the races as its official policy. Indeed, after the World Council of Churches had roundly condemned the theological basis for apartheid in 1961, the NGK had withdrawn from the membership. Within the Afrikaner community, however, both generally and from a few figures within the Church and academia for two decades, especially through the Christian Institute's mouthpiece *Pro Veritate*, there had been strong criticism of the policies. Those concerned were given short shrift, some being ostracised and others leaving the Church and the National Party. Probably the best example is the case of Beyers Naudé, an Afrikaner minister who left the Dutch Reformed Church, denouncing its racism. In 1963 he founded the Christian Institute, aimed at uniting reformist Christians from all denominations. He was seen as a traitor by many Afrikaners.

The tide was turning, however. In 1980 eight NGK theologians expressed discontent about racism, then in 1982 123 NGK ministers published an open letter rejecting the apartheid laws and it became clear that there was a major rift between conservative and radical forces within the NG church. During the fevered public debates the NGK synod was seen as a stumbling block to change, repeatedly favouring the *status quo*. However, Frank Welsh reports that in April 1984 the western synod of the

NGK, 'the mother church in the Cape and the theological powerhouse of Stellenbosch University', urged its members 'to confess their participation in apartheid with humility and sorrow' and the moderator, Johan Heyns, proclaimed:

> There is no such thing as a white superiority or black inferiority ... all people are equal before God ... there may not be under any circumstances a political policy based on oppression, discrimination and exploitation ... the task of the church is to protest against unjust laws.

A further major turning point in the white Afrikaner churches was to be the revised position of the small but powerful and fundamentalist Gereformeerde Church. In 1970 its synod had accepted a resolution to promote the policy of geographical separation. Only fifteen years later this was rescinded, the 1985 synod stating that the Bible did not support such a resolution. Given that on the Anglican side, three years earlier, the synod of the Church of the Province of Southern Africa had stated, 'Apartheid is totally unchristian, evil and a heresy' (CPSA 1983:52), it is clear that major reinterpretations were gathering force and influence.

Yet it is interesting to reflect on how church people were thinking in the second half of the 1980s, because the future could not be foreseen. I use two essays as an indication, one by JA Loader: 'Church, Theology and Change in South Africa', published in 1985, and the other by Mandy Goedhals: 'From Paternalism to Partnership?' published in 1989. The Loader essay has been referred to earlier. Towards the end of his essay Loader indicates that the international Christian criticism and the critical churches in South Africa had created an unbearable situation, especially within the NG daughter churches. He outlines the tensions within the Afrikaans churches and states that 'divisions have widened almost beyond repair'. He concludes somewhat more optimistically, or perhaps rather with faith:

> There are still others who cannot give up hope that the inevitable and fundamental change approaching South African society will come about neither in spite of the churches nor as a victory for some churches, but as a result of churches proving how reconciliation can mould a society.

In her essay Goedhals traces the movement of the Anglican Church from an imperial and paternalistic role from 1848 onwards, respectively through being the church of the government establishment and through its missionary work, to significant changes in the later decades of the twentieth century. She shows that whilst, during the first decades of apartheid, some leaders and laity protested in actions and words, the overall role of the Anglican Church was one of gradualism and of protest, rather than resistance. She echoes the view of Loader that a fair proportion of the white Christian laity were very sensitive as to how they would fare with the ending of apartheid.

Be that as it may, it is very clear that pressure was building up within the faith systems, amongst both the leadership and the laity, making change inevitable. Quoting from Religious Faith and Anti-Apartheid Activism:

> In 1988, the United Democratic Front launched a nationwide Defiance Campaign in which religious activists of all faiths were prominent once again, despite the threats of banning, intimidation, torture, criminal prosecution and even death. They, along with hundreds of liberation activists, helped mount the intense pressure on the government that led to the 1990 negotiations between the leaders of the National Party and the African National Congress.

It is likely that a key factor in the change was the growing influence of the South African Council of Churches, of which Bishop Tutu was general secretary from 1978 to 1984. It is said that Tutu, later to become the Archbishop in Cape Town, refused to isolate theology and religion from politics; he saw these as converging and inextricable. In a sense this is hardly surprising given the mission and teachings of Christ, something conveniently and duly forgotten over the centuries as some churches identified themselves with the government in power.

In conclusion, the question arises about the role of the spirit of ubuntu in unravelling apartheid and over the last twenty years. In November 2011, when I was chatting to a doorman outside a Cape Town hotel, something happened needing his patience and I said to him that he had demonstrated ubuntu. He said, 'Yes, we have got that from Mandela.'

To explain, ubuntu is an ancient religious philosophy of African people, which precedes their introduction to Christianity but, significantly, reflects some of the major Christian tenets. Ubuntu sees lives to be based on values such as the communal spirit, kindness, compassion, forgiveness, and respect for creation, animate and inanimate. These are the values which make human beings 'human' and which enable a judgement to be reached about a person at the day of judgement, when one meets the ancestors. Desmond Tutu is said to have brought together the spirit of ubuntu and Christianity into a new theology, which incorporates the communalism of ubuntu and the individualist responsibility of the Christian ethic. Linked to this is the Tutu perception of Jesus Christ as a fighter for the poor and the unprivileged and the outcast, who preached against power and privilege and pursued tenets such as 'do as you would be done by' as a form of political action.

Interestingly, the final section of the Constitution of South Africa, quoting from it:

> provides an historical bridge between the past of a deeply divided society characterised by strife, conflict, untold suffering and injustice, and a future founded on the recognition of human rights, democracy and peaceful co-existence and development opportunities for all South Africans, irrespective of colour, race, class, belief or sex.

It goes on to require that the wrongs of the past 'can now be addressed on the basis there is a need for understanding but not for vengeance, a need for reparation but not retaliation, a need for ubuntu but not for victimisation'. This was the basis for the work of the Truth and Reconciliation Commission, which was to be a very fitting tribute to the constructive thinking of Mandela and Tutu and which is penetratingly analysed and assessed by Father Michael Lapsley in his book *Redeeming the Past*.

Sport and Apartheid

ونونو

One Monday in March 2014 in Cape Town we went to the Sahara Cricket Ground in Newlands, famous not only for the towering presence of Table Mountain but also for the adjacent Castle Brewery. It was the fourth day of the test match between South Africa and Australia. To be frank, much as we love Australia and the Australians, the humiliation of England by Australia in the recent tour led us to support the Springboks, to no avail of course as the day went by. Nevertheless, we had a wonderful day, with brilliant weather and a great sense of occasion. We left the ground with very happy memories.

The South African team featured different races. The days were long gone, therefore, from the 1890s when Krom Hendricks, a gifted coloured player, had been denied a place in provincial and national South African teams, or much later the furore surrounding Basil D'Oliveira in the 1960s, which is covered later in this sketch. The crowd in 2014 was completely multi-racial, the people very much at ease with each other. The grassy banks were occupied by families of all colours, watching, laughing and picnicking. The attendants, taking tickets, guiding and vending, were happy to be there, having a good rapport with the customers. During the match there was the usual loud ribaldry, laughter and groans as events unfolded. Amazingly, for somebody used to test matches in England, the lunch break involved an innovation. Ground staff came out and fenced off the square and then several thousand spectators flocked onto the ground, to look at the square, to wander and chat together, to play cricket on the outfield, even with stumps, and to run and chase. This was a great and happy and unexpected scene.

At the end of the day we left in an orderly way, good humoured despite the drubbing in sight for South Africa. There was not a hint of aggravation or violence during the whole day. We were fascinated and charmed and the day brought to mind how important sport has been and is to South Africa, and how damaging to the national psyche and existence the sporting sanctions against South Africa must have been.

Whilst the tendency has been to concentrate on the apartheid era, from 1948 to 1991, as the main culprit for apartheid in sport, it is only fair to

Lunchtime, Sahara Park

indicate that the racial approach to sport went back many decades and did not relate only to the Afrikaners! For example, Krom Hendricks was denied a place touring to England with the South African team in 1894 because of the decisions of the white English-speaking cricket establishment in Cape Town. Yet this racial approach was not confined to 'whites' in relation to 'blacks'. We are told that the Ottoman CC, a Muslim club in Cape Town, turned down an application from Basil D'Oliveira, a Roman Catholic, to join them when he was a teenager. This reminds me of my days playing cricket in Hong Kong in 1950 when, in the second division of the Hong Kong Cricket League, our King George V School played the Indian Recreational Club, the Chinese Recreational Club and the Club de Recreio, amongst other teams. However, I was unaware of any racial aspect to this, our own school team being happily multi-ethnic, including two Indians, two Chinese, an Australian, an American, a New Zealander, a Czech and three British.

Our experience on that day in March 2014 was nearly a quarter of a century after the formal abandonment of apartheid in sport in South Africa and the ending of international sanctions. Apartheid policies had banned multi-racial sport and South Africa's growing isolation from world sport began in the mid-1950s. In South Africa white and non-white people were to organise their own leagues, and there were to be no mixed-race teams and no interracial competition. This meant also that visiting teams were unable to use non-white players, and this excluded many national teams across a wide spectrum of sport from visiting South Africa.

Obviously there had to be a response from the world sporting bodies, and this came in stages, sport by sport, as described by ES Reddy in 'Sports and the liberation struggle'. In 1956 the International Table Tennis Federation cut its ties to the all-white South African Table Tennis Union, indicating that it would deal with the non-racial South African Table Tennis Board. The riposte of the apartheid government was to withdraw the passports of the Board's players! In 1963 South Africa was suspended by the Federation of International Football Associations and it was barred from the 1964 Olympic Games in Tokyo. 1970 saw the South African National Olympic Committee expelled from the International Olympic Committee, a South African cricket tour to England cancelled, and South Africa banned from tennis's Davis Cup and also from international athletics. To cap it all, in 1970 an All Blacks rugby tour included Maoris who were given the status of honorary white people, which caused such an uproar in New Zealand that the following 1973 Springbok tour of New Zealand had to be cancelled.

South Africa had been excluded from the World Rugby Union Cup finals in 1987 and was to be again in 1991. This makes more remarkable and symbolic the Rugby Union World Cup triumph of South Africa in Cape Town in 1995, which I return to later. Even the Formula 1 South African Grand Prix was affected when the International Federation cancelled future races following 1985.

In stages the whole of South African sport was damaged to a greater or lesser extent by these developments, apart from golf. White players increasingly could get no international competition in sports teams representing South Africa, and the huge reservoir of black, coloured and Asian talent could not be developed, whilst ardent sports fans in South Africa for decades were denied the thrill of receiving and watching other national teams.

Concerning golf, the most remarkable incident occurred when an Indian golfer, Sewsunker 'Papwa' Sewgolum, won the Natal Open Golf Championship. Already he had won the Dutch Open in 1959 and 1960, but here in Natal, he had to receive the trophy through a clubhouse window in the pouring rain, and as a non-white he was not allowed into the clubhouse to join the usual celebrations. Moreover, he was banned from all South African major tournaments after 1963. This sort of happening makes nonsense of statements such as the one by Reg Honey, the South African International Olympic Committee representative in 1960: 'There's no racial discrimination in South African sport, it's all lies, it's just that there are no blacks fit to take part in the Olympics.' What an irony this is as we note the increasing dominance of Caribbean and other black sprinters in the Olympic Games!

An interesting and very relevant case study about these times concerns Basil D'Oliveira, a very talented all-round cricketer. Of Portuguese and Indian extraction, he was born in Signal Hill, Cape Town, in 1931. Showing tremendous promise as a teenager, as a 'coloured' he was denied the opportunity to play first-class cricket, being confined to the non-white weekend leagues and working during the week in a printworks. One perspective on this is in *Basil D'Oliveira, Cricket & Conspiracy: The Untold Story*, a brilliant book by Peter Oborne: 'White people got access to the best pitches, the best facilities, the best coaching and international recognition. Basil D'Oliveira was obliged to play his cricket on patches of scrubland and semi-desert around Cape Town'. However, his talent had been spotted early on, especially by John Arlott, the revered English cricket commentator, who later persuaded the Lancashire league club of Middleton to employ him in 1960. The invitation and the offer of a wage did not come with the fare to travel, but a huge effort was made in Cape Town by the non-white community to raise the money, so much did this invitation mean to that community. It was seen as a breakthrough, that 'one of theirs' could make professional cricket in England.

By 1966 D'Oliveira was playing for England, having moved success-fully to county cricket with Worcestershire in 1963. His progress, as a non-white South African, now a naturalised Briton, playing in the England test team, was to cause major ructions and to have wide impli-cations. The government of South Africa was desperate to prevent D'Oliveira from playing for England in the tour to South Africa scheduled for 1968/69. Whilst overall his 1968 summer in English cricket had been less successful than in previous years, he had enabled England to win the final match at the Oval and thereby to draw the Ashes series. In the first innings he made 158, coming in at number six when the score was four for 238; he left the crease a little over five hours later, having faced 325 balls and scored twenty-one fours. In the second Australian innings he proved his all-round worth by taking one wicket for one, a middle order batsman, in bowling five overs. To the English public, his huge fan base in South Africa and much of the press 'commentariat' his selection for the South African tour seemed inevitable, but this was not to be the case.

Oborne describes in detail the machinations through the 1967/68 period, centring on the determination of the South African government that the England touring team should not include a coloured player, and seemingly arising directly from Mr Vorster, the Prime Minister. These included contact through South African intermediaries with well-placed people sympathetic to 'white South Africa' in the Marylebone Cricket Club, a threat to withdraw the tour invitation, the offer of a fat coaching contract to D'Oliveira if he would make himself unavailable for selection, and even a sense of bribery and threat.

D'Oliveira was not selected, supposedly on cricketing grounds, during a six-hour selection meeting, the minutes of which have gone missing. Mayhem followed. The adverse commentary is best summarised by quotes from John Arlott's column in the Guardian (29 August 1968):

> MCC have never made a sadder, more dramatic, or potentially more damaging selection than in omitting D'Oliveira from their team to tour South Africa ... There is no case for leaving him out on cricketing grounds ... It could have such repercussions on British relations with coloured races in the world that the cancellation of a cricket tour would seem a trifling matter compared with the apparent British acceptance of Apartheid.

D'Oliveira, not in the chosen sixteen, had been marked down as a reserve and when Tom Cartwright did not pass a fitness test on 16 September, he was promptly invited to join the tour party. Within a week the MCC called off the tour, which clearly now would be unwelcome. This was made clear by Prime Minister Vorster, who saw the MCC as a leftist body taking its orders from Harold Wilson, the Labour Prime Minister. Oborne quotes that Vorster denounced the 'leftist and liberalist politicians who tried to twist sport for their own purposes and pink ideals', a somewhat hypocritical statement in all the circumstances.

It took another twenty years before conclusions could begin to be drawn that there were signs of a way forward. Finally, the abolishment in June 1991 of the Population Registration Act, a cornerstone of apartheid, pointed to a new future. In South Africa, the historian Welsh reports that the introduction of non-racial sport was obviously on the way when 'the rugby team of the coloured Paulus Joubert High School at Paarl could play the famous Africaner Paarl Gymnasium, and beat them'. A sign of complete easing of international restrictions followed with the European Community's announcement of the ending of the boycott in June 1991, and shortly afterwards India lifted its ban on playing South Africa at cricket. For the sports-loving people of South Africa these must have been great blessings, something we sensed during our own special day at Sahara Park in Cape Town.

On to the occasion of sports awards at Tuynhuys on 16 May 1995, as the President of South Africa, Nelson Mandela, in heralding the forthcoming World Rugby Union Cup, was able to say:

> With the acceptance of democratic South Africa into international sport and the achievements of our teams and individuals, we have developed a new spirited patriotism. Our national teams now enjoy the support of all South Africans. This new and fresh approach amongst our people has enhanced the Government of National Unity's efforts to build a new South African nation. It is an approach that should be rewarded with an acceleration of the movement towards the day when all our teams shall be truly representative of our people.

Compare this with a statement by South African Prime Minister Vorster some three decades earlier, quoted by Oborne:

> Over my dead body will we allow a black man, a coloured man, an Indian man to become a Springbok, whether it be in rugby, cricket, football, you name it.

It is fitting, therefore, to review the symbolic and moving occasion on 24 June 1995 when the Springboks won the World Rugby Union Cup. Rugby had been seen to be 'a Boer game', a symbol of white supremacy. Earlier Nelson Mandela had given his blessing to the squad, all but one of them being white, at their training ground. Meredith writes that Mandela stated:

> [W]e have adopted these young men as our boys, as our own children, as our own stars. This country is fully behind them. I have never been

so proud of our boys as I am now and I hope that that pride we all share.

On the cup final day in Cape Town Mandela wore the Springbok cap, and the number 6 jersey of the Springbok captain, Francois Pienaar. Meredith describes how after a tremendous victory in extra time against the All Blacks, an overwhelmingly white crowd burst 'into a frenzy of enthusiasm and excitement' and 'the whole of South Africa erupted in celebration, blacks as joyful as whites'. Back in the UK we sensed that this great and momentous time of national fusion was shared emotionally around the world by those who wished the rainbow nation well.

Two quotations, drawn from the SportsPro article 'History of Sport – South Africa emerges from its dark past', are poignant and revealing. From Joost van der Westhuizen, the Springboks' scrum-half:

I think the best thing was to see him in a Springbok jersey ... it was a total surprise. Then we realised the whole country was behind us, and for this man to wear a Springbok jersey was a sign, not just for us, but for the whole of South Africa, that we have to unite and we have to unite today.

And from Tokyo Sexwale, a powerful former anti-apartheid activist:

Only Mandela could wear an enemy jersey. Only Mandela would go down and be associated with the Springboks. The liberation struggle of our people was not just about liberating blacks from bondage, but more so it was about liberating white people from fear. And there it was. Fear melting away. People were shouting, 'Nelson! Nelson!' And who were these people, these rugby crowds? They were our jailers, our oppressors; the people guarding the borders, the police stations. But it was, 'Nelson! Nelson!' We stood there and we did not know what to say ... You sat there and knew it was worthwhile. All the years underground, in trenches, denial, self-denial, away from home, prison; it was worth it. For truly that day we supped with the gods.

What a change this was, and twelve years later the Springboks again won the Rugby World Cup in Paris, their flying black winger, Bryan Habana, a scorer of eight tries in the tournament, being awarded International Rugby Board Player of the Year.

*

This sketch closes with some reflections by two of our grandsons, Fergus and Ben Pickles, on their experience in Western Cape Province. Fergus travelled on the August 2013 Pate's Grammar School rugby tour, whilst Ben followed a year later with the Cheltenham College rugby tour, and each tour consisted of five matches. I was interested to learn about the teams they had played against and the conditions played in. As I mentioned to them, a quarter of a century earlier, it is doubtful that they would have got to South Arica to play. First, their schools may have been disinclined to send teams to an apartheid-dominated South Africa, and parents might not have been all that keen to support such tours either. Second, presumably they would only have been able to play 'white' school teams. My question to them, therefore, was 'what did you find?'

Fergus Pickles, who also spent two months working in Johannesburg townships in the winter of 2014, wrote as follows:

For me the issue is no longer one of race but of class. In my experience nobody involved in sport in South Africa had any kind of prejudice about who they would or wouldn't play with, and when on tour there every side I played against had a mix of Afrikaner, English and Black players, along with occasional Indians. My guess though

Cricket in Ocean View

would be that if you looked at the top schools they are far more dominated by richer white children – the best side that we played had far fewer non-whites. I think the key word here is rich, rather than white. Nobody cares about the skin colour of these players, but the wealth gap in South Africa remains so extensively dominated by colour, merely as a residue of the inequality of apartheid, that it is just far more unlikely for non-white players to make it. Ultimately there isn't going to be a sudden groundswell of international class black players without significant investment into sports development in black communities.

The comments of Ben Pickles are interesting in another way, with some selected quotes:

> During our Cheltenham College rugby tour to South Africa we played Wynberg Boys' High (winning 15–6), Bergvliet High School (22–3), Lagunya RFC (58–0), Paarl Boys' High (losing 7–38) and Grey College Port Elizabeth (losing 15–58). The first two schools were in Cape Town and had fairly similar cultures shown in both teams, with a few exceptions. Wynberg featured a predominantly white group but perhaps three black boys. This team was fairly large in size and played on a beautiful pitch ... The team at Bergvliet was fairly similar, however much smaller in size and also very white in origin. They too played on a well-kept pitch, which was in very good condition. Next we played the Lagunya RFC Township team, which was a completely different experience. All of the boys were black with no exception, and played a different brand of rugby which was fast flowing. The pitch was fairly ragged, however not too bad – it did require a quick mind before the match to ensure there were no sharp objects such as rocks on the pitch – we did find a couple. The physical condition of the boys wasn't as good as the other teams we had played so far, but it was expected, considering the difference in funding between the schools. The next two teams we played were on a completely different level. They were both fantastic rugby schools – the sport living deep in their culture. Both teams boasted physical dominance and skill, which we found difficult to compete with. As for the origins of the boys, Paarl were all white and spoke Afrikaans amongst each other, whereas the previous teams all spoke English as their first language. Grey College Port Elizabeth were also white in the majority, but they did have four black boys in their team.

It is relevant that on 3 January 2016 our family in England was watching a day of test cricket between South Africa and England at Sahara Park on Sky Sports. During the lunch interval there was a revealing film about the Gary Kirsten Foundation, more details of which feature in Part III of this book. The film focused on the work of the foundation in the Cape Town township of Khayelitsha in bringing cricket coaching opportunities to impoverished children, and the head teacher of the Chris Hani High School was interviewed.

The point was made that since the return of South Africa to the international cricket fold, only seven black South Africans had played for the Proteas. To look more positively at this result after twenty-two years of post-apartheid cricket in South Africa: twenty-five years ago, not one black or coloured person could have played for their country. Now, in the January of 2016, Temba Bavuma, aged twenty-five and born in Langa Township, has become the first black cricketer to score a century, and it helped to save the innings of South Africa in the second test against England at Sahara Park in Cape Town. As reported by Jonathan Agnew on BBC Sport, this innings 'transcended cricket' and 'he batted absolutely brilliantly and was a breath of fresh air', whilst the *Cape Argus* reported, 'Bavuma now the toast of the nation'.

Part II
The Flats

The home of much of the population of Greater Cape Town.

The Cape Flats

⌒⌒⌒

The Cape Flats are an extensive crescent-shaped area of land lying between the Cape Peninsula in the west and south and the Hottentots Holland Mountains in the north and east. Topographically, one sees a large plain, but with rising ground at the foot of the Cape Peninsula in the west and more rising ground towards the mountains in the north and east. In the south-east the Cape Flats merge into the broad sweeping sandy beaches covering much of the shoreline of False Bay, which extend towards Somerset West. The Flats lie close to the Atlantic in the west and abut False Bay and the Indian Ocean in the east. The size is 25 kilometres from east to west and 15 from north to south, an estimated 375 square kilometres.

Cape Peninsula used to be an island, but over two millennia a vast sheet of wind-blown Aeolian sand has formed the Flats to join the peninsula to the mainland. Most of the sand is unconsolidated in the Flats, but some older dunes have been consolidated into soft sandstone. The power of the onshore winds from the south-east to pick up sand from the beaches and carry it far inland was demonstrated to us during several afternoons. People were being driven from the beach and the outside restaurant tables by smothering wind-blown sand at Fish Hoek. Driving from there to Simon's Town took us through a sandstorm especially heavy in the Glencairn area, where winds blowing from the beach over the centuries had driven sand inland to form large dunes. Late in 2015 the coastal rail link between Simon's Town and Muizenberg was closed because of drifting sand dunes.

Prior to the nineteenth century this crescent-shaped area was covered with low bushes and settled by a few hunters and collectors. It was a difficult area to trek through from Cape Town to reach the mountainous interior. The clearance of bushes for fuel worsened conditions; the windblown unconsolidated sands formed into sand dunes and intractable sheets of sand, dreadfully difficult for the oxen-led wagons to cross.

Starting in 1827 and through to the end of the century there were extensive plantings by the authorities of alien vegetation, including wattles from Western Australia and New South Wales. The initiative stabilised the dunes and drifting sands, but the invasive wattle has become a scourge. This spreading vegetation enabled permanent tracks to be established connecting Cape Town with the interior, but the Flats remained an area to go through rather than to live in, until the latter part of the nineteenth century when efforts were made to people some of the area. The acidic soils are infertile and are naturally hostile to cultivation, but they can be worked intensively through scientific soils management. This has been well illustrated by the German farmers who were encouraged in the last quarter of the nineteenth century to migrate from the sandy Lüneburg Heath in North Germany to settle in an area of the Flats, known as Die Duine ('the Dunes'), but soon to become Philippi. For several decades this was a market gardening area supplying the city, but it was to be an economy dislocated by the forced removals policies.

In recent years the strongly spreading micro-farms movement has been involving local people in making the soils produce both for the home and for sale; however, the outward urban spread of Cape Town is now threatening to take in such cultivable land. This is well illustrated by the recent furore concerning alternative uses of land in the Phillipi Horticultural Area, which sets two schools of thought against each other. On the one hand, the government of Western Cape Province and the City of Cape Town see a major need for new housing to cope with the expansion of Cape Town. On the other hand, the micro-farming and environmental lobbies see such an extension as detrimental both to the working and non-working poor, who need the land, and to the general ecology.

Cape Flats is a coastal area in the southern hemisphere on latitude 34. The climatologist sees the area to have a Mediterranean climate, reflecting the change and length of the seasons, the temperature regimes and the rainfall pattern. In the hottest month of February, the average highest daily temperature is 29°C, whilst the average lowest is 16°C; in the coolest month, July, the average highest daily temperature is 19°C and the lowest is 7°C.

What this means for the area is a long spring season merging into summer from November through to March, the average temperature approaching 30°C with the possibility of real heat from December through to February. The autumn season, from March to May, has warm sunny days, little wind, some drizzle and mildly warm nights. This is followed by the cold, windy and rainy winter months, between June and August, when cold fronts move from the north-west across the peninsula from the Atlantic Ocean, especially in August and September. The rainiest months are June to August, each with an average of sixteen rainy days, with July on average having nearly 100 mm of precipitation. The driest months are January to March, with February having on average only six rainy days and an average precipitation of 15 mm. However, as the movement of the air masses is unpredictable there are outbursts of unseasonal weather within this pattern.

What this climate means overall for dwellers in the Cape Flats is warm, dry summers and cool, damp winters, with particular exposure to strong winds from the north-west in winter and from the south-east in summer and with some unpredictability. Summer temperatures can reach 35°C but winter temperatures can range from 20 to 25°C during the day and fall to a range from 10°C to as low as -5°C at night. Conditions, therefore, for the hundreds of thousands living in the townships in 'informal' homes, can be too hot in summer and in the winter cold at night and nastily wet and windy, leading sometimes to flooding, which exacerbates problems for the dwellers there. Areas of informal homes in the townships lack piped water and for many the toilets are buckets. The poorly drained Cape Flats are the natural drainage basin for water gushing down in torrents from Table Mountain after the heavy rains. The resulting floods overtop the clogged-up drains; the flood water spreads, picking up sewage and refuse, and seeps into the shacks. The results are hunger, disease and deprivation. This is well illustrated by a Worcester Park Flood Risk Report:

> During the month of July 2007, unrelenting rains dumped over 120 millimetres of rain over a period of five days on the City of Cape Town, leading to flooding that impacted on 8000 households (38,000 residents) located primarily in the informal settlements outside the City, such as the Bongani Section of Khayelitsha and Phola Park Philippi. Such flooding is increasingly common and compromises public health and safety, destroys personal property and adversely impacts on livelihoods.

Despite efforts to relieve the situation the problems persist, as demonstrated by serious disturbances in Langa in July 2014 when rioters pressed for relief from flooding, for improved water and sanitation and for better housing.

Until the 1950s 'the Flats' were largely uninhabited, except for a few scattered farmers, but increasingly from the 1950s onwards a large area became 'apartheid's dumping ground', a wasteland designated to be occupied by non-white people. Black, coloured and Asian people were moved, in stages, to their separate areas in efforts to establish all-white sectors in Cape Town along the coast and the mountainous Table Mountain stretch. In stages new townships were established from 1955 through to the 1980s; Nyanga, Gugulethu, Ocean View, Mitchell's Plain and Khayelitsha were the main ones. Now making up Greater Cape Town, the whole area is estimated to have a population of 1.2 million.

It is interesting to see the separation of races which was established during this apartheid period. Table 2 indicates the different Black African and coloured townships and the primary language characteristics of each township. It also illustrates the very high population density, compared with some of the white areas, such as Pinelands and Newlands. On the face of it there seems to have been little change in the racial composition of the townships since the ending of apartheid. Yet there are interesting signs of change elsewhere, as illustrated by the demographic changes in the Pinelands residential area between 2001 and 2011 (Tables 3 and 4)

Table 2: Cape Flats settlements by size, race and language characteristics (2011)

Settlement	Established	Area (sq. miles)	People (to nearest 1,000)	Ethnicity %	Language %	Population density (per square mile)
LANGA	1927	1.19	52,000	Black African 99.1	Xhosa 92 English 2.5	44,000
KHAYELISTSHA	1985	15	392,000	Black African 98.6	Xhosa 90.5 English 3.2 Afrikaans 1.1	26,000
MITCHELL'S PLAIN	1970s	17	310,000	Coloured 90.8 Black African 7.3	English 47.4 Afrikaans 46.9 Xhosa 3.3	18,000
OCEAN VIEW	1969	0.68	14,000	Coloured 91.4 Black African 6.8	Afrikaans 57.2 English 39.1	20,000
NYANGA	1955	1.19	58,000	Black African 98.8	Xhosa 90.2 English 3	49,000
GUGULETHU	1960s	2.51	98,000	Black African 98.6	Xhosa 88.6 English 3.6 Afrikaans 1.7	39,000
BONTEHEUWEL	c. 1960	1.19	53,000	Coloured 94.3 Black African 4.1	Xhosa 92 English 2.5	44,000

Table 2: Cape Flats settlements by size, race and language characteristics (2011) *(continued)*

Settlement	Established	Area (sq. miles)	People (to nearest 1,000)	Ethnicity %	Language %	Population density (per square mile)
PHILIPPI	c. 1980	18.52	201,000	Black African 90.3 Coloured 8	Xhosa 78.7 Afrikaans 7.3 English 6.2	11,000
PINELANDS (adjacent to Flats)	1919	2.26	14,000	White 62.3 Black African 13.5 Coloured 15 Indian/Asian 5.1	English 81.5 Afrikaans 8.4 Xhosa 3.5	6,300
NEWLANDS (adjacent to Flats)	1660	5.19	12,000	White 82.2 Black African 9.5 Coloured 5.1	English 83 Afrikaans 12.6	2,300

Table 3: Pinelands: changes in population size and race 2001 to 2011

	2001	2011	Notes
Population total	10,618	14,198	Population increase of 34% in one decade
White %	83.5	62.3	White population down from 4/5 to 3/5 of total
Coloured %	7.79	15.1	Almost doubled
Black %	6.21	13.5	More than doubled
Indian/Asian %	2.49	5.1	More than doubled
Other %	6.21	4	

Table 4: Pinelands: changes in language 2001 to 2011

	2001	2011
Population total	10,618	14,198
English %	87	81.5
Afrikaans %	6.3	8.4
Xhosa %	3.3	3.5
Other %	2.81	6.6

The conclusion from these Pinelands tables is that in this area the previous white areas policy of the apartheid period is being eroded quickly through new building development, bigger families moving in and market forces.

Whilst conditions are unsatisfactory in many townships in the Flats there is a sense of progress being made in housing and services, but people are coming into the area from the Eastern Cape Province, Ciskei and Transkei, from the Central African countries and also from Zimbabwe, Malawi and Somalia in the hope of finding work. To these immigrants, beset by problems in their homeland, Cape Town seems to be a Mecca. However, such immigration is putting pressure on the services and causing more competition for jobs; it is extending the shanty developments and fostering dangerous tensions with the locals. The townships are oppressed with overcrowding; they suffer high unemployment, gang warfare and criminality and HIV/AIDS. The difficulties increase as they receive immigrants, many of whom extend the townships onto waste ground in building their shacks of tin, cardboard and tarpaulin. This has been a particular feature of the black townships, rather than coloured settlements such as Ocean View. The tendency has been to concentrate on these black townships, in terms of development money and foreign charity support, and there is a strong feeling within the coloured communities that they are being left behind.

All of this is reported on locally and in the international media and leads to pessimism about the future, yet more optimistic perspectives are possible. John Carlin, a well-known South African journalist, concludes:

> [T]here are two South Africas. One is uplifting, the other is frightening. One is made up of people who are unusually polite, generous, indomitable, forgiving and brave; the other of people who are reckless, volatile, violent, hot-headed.

Deon Meyer, at the end of his book *Dead Before Dying*, writes realistically about 'My South Africa' in a piece full of facts and anti-myths. In terms of progress he points to the following: between 1994 and 2011 access to clean drinking water increased from 62% to 84% and access to electricity from 24% to 84%. In 1994 only 2.5 million people had access to social grants, but by 2010 the number had reached 13.5 million, including 8.5 million children, 3.5 million pensioners and 1.5 million people with disabilities. Concerning death rates among visitors, much in the press, he indicated a much lower rate in South Africa than elsewhere, in Thailand and Germany for example.

My own optimism is based on many examples of determined self-help often supported by charities and volunteers, which encourage us about the future, and they are described in Part III of this book.

Langa Township

❦

Langa Township is a suburb of Cape Town, lying 15 kilometres to the south-east of the centre of Cape Town, almost adjacent to the international airport. It is bounded in the south by the N2 motorway, by the M7 in the east, the M17 in the west and the railway to Cape Town in the north. There is only one vehicular entrance to Langa, off the N2 via Bhunga Way, thought to have been planned long ago to enable it to be 'shut down' in times of trouble. Over the M17 to the north-west is the delightful garden village of Pinelands.

Langa stretches across part of the area to the south-east of central Cape Town known as the Cape Flats, which includes other townships such as Nyanga, Gugulethu, Khayelitsha and Mitchell's Plain. A township in South African terms is a settlement largely occupied by non-white people: black, coloured and Indian. Especially during the apartheid period, separate townships were developed and designated for the different ethnic groups. For example Langa and Khayelitsha were designated for Black Africans whilst Mitchell's Plain and Ocean View were for coloured people.

The nearest 'township' to the centre of Cape Town, Langa is the second oldest in Western Cape Province, the oldest being Ndabeni (formerly Uitvlugt), established in 1901 after an outbreak of bubonic plague in central Cape Town led to 5,000 people being moved there from dwellings in the docks area, which were viewed to be congested slums. Settlement in the Langa area started in 1918, when Africans, again being identified as a health risk, were moved there following the flu epidemic, which was having disastrous effects throughout the world. It continued in 1919 and developed further in stages during the 1920s until Langa Township was officially opened in 1927, and it has been in transition ever since through various phases of building development and the spread of informal shacks. There was more development there from 1927 onwards, following the 1923 Urban Areas Act, which declared urban areas to be 'white' and required African men in cities to carry passes. All of this shows clearly that the antecedents of the apartheid system were emerging well before 1948, when the formal apartheid period started with the National Party government.

Earlier, in 1922, land had been granted for the establishment of a formal township. It was designed, along with Pinelands and Maitland, as a garden village. However, if we look at Langa and Pinelands today, the notion of two similar garden villages ended on the drawing board. Pinelands became a village of thatched houses, whilst Langa had single-sex dormitories, observation towers and unscalable fences and was said to look more like a prison. To make the point further, these days, leafy Pinelands, with a mixed-race population of 14,000 has a population density of 6,300 per square mile, whilst the somewhat arid Langa, which is 99% Xhosa, has a population of 52,000 with a density of 44,000 per square mile. Pinelands and Langa are next to each other!

It seems that the 'garden village' design was adapted to suit what were referred to as 'African requirements' and focused on black urban workers and temporary migrants rather than permanent residents. To this end the 1924 railway sidings connected the new township to Cape Town, and the migrant workers would march up Lerotholi Avenue to the administration block to be processed, which included dipping and medical examination and the allocation of beds. Accommodation was in the main barracks, four U-shaped quadrants arranged around the central eating house. The barracks were for 2,032 single men and included eighty-four dormitories in blocks of twenty-one, each block having its own ablution and toilet facilities. Each dormitory had twenty-four bunks in double tiers and was serviced by two electric light points and one combustion stove. This first development was followed by others, including one- and two-room units, a spinsters' quarter, the North Barracks for 840 single men, a hospital, married quarters and sports ground, all completed by 1934. Another major development between 1944 and 1948 was the Old Flats, eight four-storey blocks with ablution and toilet facilities on each floor, providing for 1,296 men. The final major Second World War development was the Zones, a series of small row hostels.

Since then there have been two developments, the first being the informal settlements, stretching out into unused areas and filling niches here and there. These are made up of shacks, often of only one room, and constructed in corrugated iron, plastic, tarpaulin, wooden planks and plasterboard. There are narrow alleyways between these lines of shacks. All have electricity and many have TVs, although most are lit up by oil lamps and cooking is on charcoal-fired stoves. Water is from communal standpipes and toilets are communal also. Refuse tends to litter these areas and drainage is rudimentary. Each little building is a home, looked

Old and new in Langa

after as well as possible, and may house up to six people. The people we met were intrigued to see us but welcoming and dignified, and they seem to have an inner strength in the face of what we would see to be suffering and great poverty.

The second development has been the effort to upgrade the existing houses and the hostels and, in recent years, to replace the informal settlements with permanent housing and better urban infrastructure.

Knowing this background, in February 2014 we drove 20 kilometres from our rented apartment in Fish Hoek, above the Jaeger Walk overlooking False Bay. Our mission was to visit Langa Township to continue our work to understand and to support pre-schools in the area. At the back of our minds was the *Cape Town Stories* book project, and what I would be writing about the Langa Township. How can one adequately relate to and describe such a township and do it justice, how can one begin to understand what life can be like there?

We joined the N2, and left at Junction 12. We drove over a bridge along the only road access to Langa and down a gentle slope into Bungha Way with the township ahead of us on either side of the road.

It is wrong for this township to be described solely in terms of the former infamous singles quarters, the sprawling informal shacks of squatters and a vast taxi rank. Yes, there are such sights, and they are very moving, for example to visiting Europeans, but these are within and adjacent to permanent buildings in bricks and plastered blocks.

We are reminded that one of our Xhosa guides had said that Langa is socially diverse 'with an upper, middle and lower class'. The evidence of this is in the variety of housing of the people. The single-storey buildings vary from smallish ranch-style homes to semi-detached and terraced homes, and there are the hostels referred to above.

Most of the roads are for two-way traffic, they are tarmac-covered and have verges, paths and kerbs. Many of the roads are partly tree-lined but the verges are of very sparse grass, with sandy soil dominating. Although there is not much vehicular traffic, there are plenty of pedestrians about and the area seems to be buzzing. There is an air of neglect about most of these roads and paths, with weeds growing up alongside the kerbs and a scattering of refuse. The hostel areas are separated from each other by barren ground, hardened soil, littered with bits and pieces including the inevitable plastic bags.

Many of the houses, which look well cared for, have low fences and very small gardens. Lean-to buildings are seen in some properties and in niches alongside the roads, and are used for accommodation and for small business activities. These businesses have garish and descriptive signs, crudely hand-painted, apart from a number of professional-looking signs, which are associated with a standard Coca-Cola advert. Some examples of signs include, describing exactly the building's function, 'Maribo's Hair Salon', 'African Gospel Church', 'Busy Corner', 'Langa Mini Builder', 'Siyak Hutina Educare Centre', 'Chip-Chop Tuck Shop', 'Grocer Hamper', 'Welding and burgla gate window', 'Tula's Hair Salon and Barber', and 'Kwa-Malume Cash Store'. Most of these small businesses are in temporary, home-made units in niches between buildings and along pavements. Once again planks, hardboard and corrugated iron are much used as building materials, often for single-room establishments, but there is the odd container scattered around for business, such as that of Soldiem Barber.

There are a few bigger stores, for example one for all sorts of goods including groceries and alcohol. This sort of store is heavily protected against theft and ransacking. A store I went into had iron bars at the window, barbed wire around the roof, and the cashier's area protected by a metal grid, whilst outdoors there was a heavy, vigilant security guard.

The question arises as to why all businesses are so small and makeshift. No better answer can be given than this quote from Martin Meredith:

> Black townships in 'white' South Africa were kept as unattractive as possible. Few urban amenities were ever provided. Black businessmen were prevented by government restrictions from expanding their enterprises there. No African was allowed to carry on more than one business. Businesses were confined to 'daily essential necessities', like wood, coal, milk and vegetables. No banks or clothing stores or supermarkets were permitted. Restrictions were even placed on dry-cleaners, garages and petrol stations. Nor were Africans allowed to establish companies or partnerships in urban areas, or to construct their own buildings.

Two decades after the ending of the apartheid regime there now are encouraging signs of development in Langa Township. A joint initiative by the City of Cape Town and the Nu-Hold Group involves the modernisation of Langa Railway Station and the construction, alongside it, of a new and modern shopping centre, to be opened in 2015:[1] a large

---

[1] NB: this was written prior to the Langa Junction shopping centre's opening and is updated below.

pedestrian retail development, with 'the first convenience shopping centre' in the township. Langa Station is used daily by 45,000 commuters linking to Khayelitsha and through Woodstock to the centre of Cape Town, a twenty-five-minute journey. The development of the station involves an overhead commuter pedestrian bridge to the adjacent Epping industrial area, the upgrade of the station forecourt to include soft and hard paving landscaping, the extension of the pedestrian area and the inclusion of sites for formal stalls for local traders. The Nu-Hold Group initiative is alongside the station, sharing its forecourt, and will include twelve stores, two ATM facilities, and eight smaller spaces for entrepreneurs and small and medium-sized enterprises. Land also has been reserved for later development. This retail initiative will give local people, including commuters, more choice and save the time, cash and energy they have had to spend in shopping. Langa people have been travelling by minibus to a place like Athlone, eight kilometres away, quite difficult to access and very difficult to park in, or by train to town to shop.

There is another very important aspect to this large project: the creation of immediate work opportunities and long-term employment. There is training for bricklayers and other disciplines in the building trades, thereby employing local labour. Granbuild Contracts Manager Winslow Hare stated:

> We are providing skills to the local community for plastering, bricklaying, scaffolding and ceiling installation ... Most sub-contractors will come from the local community. The specialist contractors dealing with plumbing, air conditioning and electrical will come onto the site and involve local contractors on those jobs. It is estimated that 100 jobs are being created during construction and that when finished the shopping centre will provide around 200 permanent jobs.

This is part of the transformation of Langa Township, a settlement which is relatively blessed by its proximity to Cape Town and by its location within a rail and road network. Langa Railway Station, built in 1924 to receive thousands of migrant labourers, ninety years later is becoming a hub for the economic and social transformation of the township. A marriage between the Cape Town Authority, the public sector metro line and the entrepreneurial Nu-Hold Group will help to transform Langa and the lives of many in and around the township.

*

It is now possible to update the above following my October 2015 visit. The shopping centre has been open for about six months. The two ATMs, the first in Langa, are a boon. Shoprite is making a wider variety of food available at better prices; for example, a loaf of bread is 30% cheaper than available hitherto. Shoprite attracts much custom and the car park was almost full on my visit. People are shopping here rather than trailing over to Athlone, which was expensive and time-consuming.

There are continuing signs of residential development. A major City of Cape Town Rand 151 million initiative, officially opened in 2015 by President Zuma, is the four-storey 463 residential unit apartment block development, complete with solar energy heating panels, on Bhunga Avenue next to the N2 highway.

It is in the context of these developments that decisions are being made that parts of Langa should be designated and preserved as national heritage sites. The area to be designated is the historic core of the settlement and the route taken by migrant labour from the railway station to the main barracks. The aim is to ensure that memories and values are preserved, as illustrated by government policies, settlement planning and the buildings and infrastructure. Major reactions from the people included the burning of passes in 1946, the anti-pass marches in 1960 and the 1976 student uprising. Illustrative of the ongoing historical perception of the struggle for freedom are names such as Washington Avenue (named after Booker T Washington, a nineteenth-century freed American slave), the Robert Sobukwe Memorial and Makana Square. Interestingly, after the apartheid period there can still be serious unrest at government policies, as shown by the recent serious riots relating to the intention to clear shack dwellers from the Joe Slovo area of Langa to make way for new housing development.

A simple statement about Langa as a place of high crime, with a high ratio of people with HIV/AIDS and with high unemployment, misleads us. There is dynamism, change for the better, a continuing upsurge of community work for the general good and signs of public investment and private enterprise.

The best example has developed in stages over the last fifteen years and it is the Guga S'thebe Arts and Cultural Centre, which is an important hub within Langa Township. It provides programmes in music, drama, visual art, photography and cultural clothing. It has a thriving pottery workshop, designing and firing ornamental pottery and tableware for both the local and foreign markets. It has a standing exhibition of paintings, carvings and craft goods, with all the items for sale. It includes a business centre providing for IT training and other business skills development and also a range of equipment and services to support local small businesses.

The very exciting latest initiative has been the construction of the Guga S'thebe Theatre, a multinational project involving the local community, the Cape Town Department of Arts and Culture, the architects RWTH Aachen, PBSA Dusseldorf, Georgia Tech Atlanta and the University of Cape Town. The aim is to give better facilities to the community and visiting performers and lecturers. It is a double-decked structure, with a large open space in the centre and smaller rooms around the side; being added are a recording studio, indoor and outdoor stages, and changing rooms. The double-storey theatre structure, with a capacity of 200, was constructed using eleven shipping containers, recycled wooden crates, and the straw and clay used to regulate temperature in the container building. This innovative project, involving the skills of the architect and the engineer, foreign universities and firms, volunteers and local labour, is a proud effort to continue the transformation of Langa Township.

This story can end on a still more optimistic note following the exploits of Temba Bavuma, batting at Sahara Park to reach a match-saving century, the first by a black South African. Along with Malusi Siboto and Thami Tsolekile, all of them born in the same street in Langa, he is one of the seven black players in the national cricket team in the post-apartheid years. A product of the Langa Cricket Club, for which he played at the age of thirteen, Bavuma, with the other two stars, took part in the second annual cricket festival at the Club in December 2015, the publicity stating that 'we now celebrate these [and other local] players while we inspire the younger generation that will take over from them and who better to celebrate with than the community that brought them up?'

Innovative use of containers

An Unsung Hero

࿇

At a service in St Margaret's Anglican Church in Fish Hoek, we heard a riveting sermon, which focused on 'the dash'. This arose from a poem by Linda Ellis and centred on the gravestone, which carries the name of the deceased and his/her date of birth and date of death separated by a dash. What does that dash say or hide about the life of that person?

This got me thinking about the life of Clarence Mahamba. We first met Clarence in November 2011 on our second visit to the Dalukhanyo Pre-School in Langa Township. Clarence is the chairman and we have met him several times since then. It is clear to us that he is a much respected veteran and we have been greatly impressed by his dignity, courtesy and commitment. As time went by we came to realise that he had an important story to tell and we were delighted when he agreed to be interviewed in his home in Langa over two afternoons in March 2014.

How can one capture over three hours, with a few other reference points, the life of a person? With some humility I have tried to do this.

Clarence was born in 1937 in the small town of Tsolo in Eastern Cape. He is a Xhosa of the Mpondomise tribe. He did not have much schooling but referred to some attendance at a school in the grounds of a local church. When asked, therefore, how he had learnt English so well, he replied that he had gone to night schools in Cape Town.

Having gone to stay in Johannesburg at the age of nineteen, he soon left and in 1956 arrived searching for work in Cape Town, where he had relatives in Langa. Apart from a year in the local cement factory, the main feature was a working life in hotels, boarding houses and the university within and around Cape Town, in areas including Rosebank, Muizenberg and Sea Point, where he worked in the kitchens, in porterage and general duties. During this time he married and had four children; he now has eight grandchildren. He finally retired in 1995, at the age of fifty-eight.

Much of Clarence's working life (1956 to 1995) was during the apartheid period and was completely conditioned by the requirements of this regime. These were covered by statutes relating to population registration, mixed marriages, reservation of separate amenities, group areas, and passbooks. All of these were to affect where Clarence could live, where and when he could work, and where he could go.

Particularly we chatted with him about the passbooks, which he needed to have until the system was abandoned in 1986; one of Clarence's passbooks features on this book cover. The passbook had to be carried by the black population when outside their homelands or their other designated areas. The aim was to control living and movement in the 'white areas' of South Africa. Employment granted the qualification to live in Cape Town for successive periods of six months. This needed to be vouched

Clarence Mahamba

for by the employer, who had to be white and would need to sign the passbook each month. The system was rigorous and thoroughly monitored by the police, who at their discretion could check anybody at any time. The passbook always had to be carried and to be authorised as up-to-date, otherwise a prison sentence of up to five years was inevitable.

Clarence experienced, and fought against, the rigours of the separation of men from their wives and families, as reflected in the prevalence of crowded 'men only' hostels in the townships. Movingly, reported in an article in the Cape Herald in November 1985, 'Bishop Patrick Matolengwe questioned the nature of a government which prevented a man from living with his wife and family' and said it could lead to adultery. Once again the system was ruthlessly implemented; for example, one lady told us, 'We used to be driven off from our menfolk by the police and their dogs.'

Clarence experienced all of this at first hand and worked first within the trade union movement to try to ameliorate conditions. He was an active member and finally chairman of the Liquor and Catering Workers' Union. Later this amalgamated with other small unions to form the large South African Commercial and Catering Workers' Union, which he stayed with until 1984.

Arising out of his community involvement, his trade union experience and his local stature, he was asked to take the lead in forming a special movement separate from the trade union to fight for the rights of hostel dwellers. In the rigorous times of apartheid it was considered sensible that this movement should not be seen to be involved with trade unions or political parties, some of which in any case were illegal, and he resigned from the trade union to press forward with the hostel movement. This movement was part of the wider black consciousness development, the Western Cape Civic Association having been launched in 1982. However, in his paper SE Mxokozeli states that 'most of the hostel people did not regard themselves as part of the Western Cape communities as they were mostly migrant labourers from the homelands'. Indeed, he claims that this 'resulted in conflicts with some people from the established townships. The hostels committees – the *Ntlalontle* – were structured in ways that could be considered to be an extension of the system of oppression.'

The setting up of the West Cape Men's Hostels Association (WCMHA) in 1984, with Clarence Mahamba as its first chairman, was an important initiative in bringing hostel dwellers into the wider political movement in

Comrade Mahamba

the townships. Quoting from the Cape Town Press: 'Almost a thousand migrant workers gathered in and around the Presbyterian Church Hall (St Francis) in Langa on Saturday to register their support for the founding of the first community organisation geared primarily to fight for the rights of migrant workers in the black townships', the number of whom was estimated to be 25,000. 'The launch was attended by representatives of various trade unions, churches, community bodies, the Azanian People's Organisation, the Black Sash and local universities.'

Later, in 1986, at a two-day conference attended by 300

people, Mr Mahamba, the chairman of what, with the addition of women, was now the West Cape Hostel Dwellers' Association (WCHDA), was reported as saying that hostel dwellers 'were amongst the most oppressed people in South Africa and that their living conditions were often akin to those of animals in a zoo, and he asked why it was necessary to separate husbands from their wives'. It was reported in the press that representatives from Kuils River, Strand, Stellenbosch, Nyanga, Langa and Gugulethu resolved 'to work with other progressive organisations to expand WCHDA countrywide; that the upgrading of the hostels was the main focus of the association; to work for the end of the migrant labour system; that the Government should recognise community organisations; they should support a living wage campaign and work alongside squatter communities', and 'the Conference called for the unconditional release of jailed trade unionist Oscar Mpetha, who is regarded as the father of the trade union movement in Western Cape'.

Clarence provided us with a list of pivotal events during the eight-year period which followed the founding of the WCMHA. In 1986 on 1 May there was the abolishment of the contract labour system, on 1 July there was integration of the men with the women to form WCHDA, and on 1 October the WCHDA Health Project was launched. There was a mobile clinic coupled with community outreach programmes and home visits. Primary health care, early childhood and pre-school projects followed.

In 1987 on 1 May the West Cape Hostels Trust was launched. In 1988 there was the first approach to authorities for land, whilst in 1989 the first full-time staff were employed, a pilot building project was agreed, and there was a move towards the integration of civic structures. In 1990 there was movement forming the Hostel Dwellers' Trust and then the Section 21 Utility Company, the Umzamo Development Project (a housing and social development project), and in 1991 project committees were established (LaguNya). During this period Clarence led the community movement and was part of the high-powered delegation which met with the National Party Minister of Housing, Hernus Kriel, in July 1991. He felt that the minister seemed 'scared' but during the meeting the atmosphere changed with an understanding of the West Cape Hostels movement and its aims. This was affirmed later by a government grant of Rand 10.7 million for the project.

An appreciative commentary by SE Mxokozeli states: 'The WCHDA played a pivotal role in getting the hostel communities to be part of the struggle against apartheid. They also played a big role in forging peace efforts in times of turmoil. Lack of major conflicts between the hostel communities and the established townships can be attributed among other factors to the existence of WCHDA, as they were all part of the progressive movement in the fight against apartheid domination.'

We asked Clarence whether he had experienced problems with the authorities and the police during his active period. He had, and such an answer was unsurprising. Given the paranoia of the national government, its repressive system and its suspicion of conspiracy, any person seen as being part of an association of non-white people, especially if in the lead, would be on their radar. In fact as early as 1961 the police had turned up at his home town in Eastern Province, wanting to see him. The headman had directed them to one of his brothers, a sort of red herring which did not please the brother!

Particularly memorable was the time in 1976 when he had been introduced to speak at a meeting of around 200 people at which he was secretly tape-recorded. Getting up the next morning at 4am to go to work he found the police outside, but he managed to persuade them that the one they wanted had left for work. By the time he got to his workplace the police had been there and gone off. His Afrikaner employer gave him what turned out to be wise advice: 'Present yourself voluntarily at the police station, because this will count in your favour.' Clarence duly followed this advice but at the station claimed that he could not answer their questions because he understood neither Afrikaans nor English. To his astonishment a white policemen was brought in who spoke perfect Xhosa, having been brought up on a farm with Xhosas. The tape recording was then produced, which was seen to prove that he had spoken provocatively. He claimed, however, that his statement about 'the power of the people being together' was solely to do with living conditions and was not politically connected. He was challenged as to whether he hated white people and was able to rebut this. The police decided to study the constitution of the group behind the meeting, following which he was released. They did keep an eye on him for a while, following him to check his whereabouts, but with time they lost interest in him.

The early 1980s were a time of growing dissent and more influential anti-apartheid initiatives. In the townships community associations were springing up to press for better conditions. The press was getting bolder and reporting the discontent and the campaign issues. As reported by Martin Meredith: 'in 1983 a coalition of more than 300 organisations – church groups, civic associations, trade unions and student bodies –

launched the United Democratic Front to oppose [discriminatory] constitutional changes, in what amounted to the broadest display of public opposition to apartheid in nearly thirty years. Cutting across lines of class and colour, the UDF demanded a united, democratic South Africa free from homelands and group areas.' It was against this background that Clarence Mahamba and his comrades were moving forward in Langa and other townships, and what followed is not surprising.

In 1985 there was another major incident, this being at the time of Clarence's transfer from trade union to wider community activities. The Hostel Dwellers' Office was raided and Clarence, Johnson Mkoba and others were locked up for a couple of days. The police thought that their activities were provoking people to be aggressive and this seemed to be proved by the fact that the police station was surrounded by a very large and increasingly hostile crowd. The police had a neat way out: turning to Clarence, saying that he had said that he did not want violence. If he could prove this by dispersing the crowd they would let him go, which he did, so they were released.

However, these were highly dangerous times and the leaders, including Clarence, were walking a tightrope, as was proven in 1992. Clarence had just resigned as chairman when, on 27 February, there was an attempt on the life of his successor, Lucas Mbene, who died several days later. A meeting was to be held in Nyanga and Clarence also had been due to be there, but he had missed the transport; the new chairman went alone and was shot three times. Later in 1993, on 27 June, the secretary of SANCO, Mr Nkatazo, walking to a meeting in Langa around 5pm, was bundled into a car and his body was found the next day on waste ground. No people were ever brought to trial for the murders, but suspicions are boundless concerning 'spies, informers and hired assassins'.

Clarence remains active for the pre-school movement in Langa. He is approached often to get more involved. He has been told that because of his past work he qualifies for a 'veteran's pension'. The ANC would like him to get involved in the community again, to tell them what he has done and to show how representative organisations can be built up, indicating, 'You made it all happen in the old days; show us how to do this today.' It seems that he is shortly to be involved in tutorial work, but at the age of seventy-eight he does not feel he has the capacity to do more.

Reflecting, he feels the change is unbelievable from what was experienced over so many decades, a change he and many others felt would never happen. He comments warmly on the support from politicians such as Helen Suzman and her party, from national and local church leaders, and from universities and the press, which all helped to change the climate for the work of unions and community bodies.

Clarence had never felt that there could be any other than a National Party government. People were afraid and felt that anti-government activity wasted time because there never would be a change of government. Whilst he had worked so long for change, he was 'shocked' by the rapid transitions from 1991 onwards, leading to the freeing of Nelson Mandela and the national elections with universal suffrage in 1994.

The way forward immediately after 1991 was not to be easy, as shown by the murders indicated earlier. My wife and I have reflected often on how it was that Clarence Mahamba could come unscathed through those difficult and dangerous times, when he was so active and clearly under such close scrutiny. We have decided that his personal charm, his modesty, sincerity and natural gentleness, combined with his persistent and courageous work for a right cause, must have carried him through, as he met some tough characters and very tricky situations. Perhaps on the way there also was some luck!

Pam, in Fish Hoek in March 2014, wrote as follows: 'I'm full of admiration for people like Clarence, who seem to have many things in life stacked against them, but come out with our full admiration for the way they live their lives as examples for us all and how we should live our lives.'

One Day in Langa Township
by Venerable Malcolm Lesiter

⌒⌒⌒

The trip to South Africa with Gordon and Pam Gaddes, superbly arranged and organised by Gordon, included, among many other things, visiting the Waterfront, Table Mountain, Robben Island, St George's Cathedral, the Kirstenbosch Gardens and a few days in the wine-growing area in Stellenbosch, but the most memorable day of all was the day spent in Langa Township.

The four of us were collected from our Cape Town hotel by a people-carrier and a driver who was with us for the whole day. Gladstone, our guide and driver, was a mine of information, a proud resident of Langa and a person who lived and served the culture of the township. He was only too glad to answer our questions, opening up for us the story of the townships and the life they sustained.

The day had been arranged in association with Uluntu Africa, and it became clear during the day just how much networking enables projects to flourish and how essential are formal and informal partnerships in responding to the huge challenges.

The main reason for our coming to South Africa was a visit to the Dalukhanyo Pre-School. But first we drove out to Khayelitsha, the largest Cape Town township and some 20 miles from the city, to which the suburban railway has recently been extended.

The population of Khayelitsha (1.2 million) is more than ten times that of Langa and the scale of the township is overwhelming. Our first stop was the Abalimi Community Project, a project which takes in fresh produce from micro-farms, and sorts, cleans and packs the vegetables for distribution to homes, hospitals and schools including Dalukhanyo Pre-School.

Before we reached the pre-school we visited a micro-farm run by a co-operative of six women, who grow vegetables for their own families and together work 50% of the farm for supply to Abalimi. The sandy soil is a challenge, so an efficient watering system is essential, together with the use of compost and manure. The farm also had a bio-fuel project which produced methane gas fed to two gas rings, making possible a soup kitchen.

And so to Dalukhanyo Pre-School, where we received an enthusiastic welcome from the teachers and from the children, most of whom were wearing the tracksuits provided by the trust – another practical initiative made in response to the need identified by the teachers and sourced locally. The children sang and danced for us and presented us, in thanks, with placards attached to string worn round their necks, showing their names and in some cases brightly coloured handprints. The 'hands' design (front row, far left) was used for the 2013 Langa Township Pre-School Christmas card.

While we were there we presented the outcome of a further practical initiative – the provision of first aid equipment and fire extinguishers.

We left the school for lunch at another Langa project called Eziko, a basic catering college. We had with us some of the staff of the pre-school and some other people who are seriously involved with it, including a representative of the Anglican Diocese of Cape Town, and we continued conversation with them and with partners from Uluntu Africa. Uluntu

Happiness in Dalukhanyo Pre-School

Attentive pre-school children

Africa had made the day possible, as mentioned before, and give considerable support to the pre-school.

We were driven first to the modern community and craft centre in the Langa Township. Here we were introduced to further training projects, the most striking being a pottery with hand-painted products of African design, and nearby a picture framing project. The centre makes possible the sale and display of work by local craftspeople and is a good stopping point for tourists visiting Langa Township.

Nearby is the Langa Museum, a renovated complex of huts used by the apartheid authorities to reinforce the passbook laws. The main space took the form of a magistrate's court, and with Pam, a former magistrate, among our number, we were able to re-enact the scenes of the time with amusement but with the underlying shame and anger at the unjust treatment which the regime perpetrated. Our understanding was enhanced by photos and displays showing demonstrations and protests, and records of the Langa story during the 1960s and 1970s.

Then we set off through the township on foot, led by Gqwetha Gladstone, our guide, who was able to tell us his own story of moving in

A Guga S'thebe pottery workshop

to his grandfather's hostel, and to show us his brother's current room. He gave us an accurate description of how a hostel was arranged, and the demanding lifestyle which it created. As soon as women were allowed to join their menfolk, the need for privacy encouraged couples to move out and construct a shack for themselves.

Our walk through the township revealed the housing conditions, which included containers which served as homes and businesses, and sometimes as temporary housing while more solid structures are slowly being built to replace the shacks which are such a feature of similar townships the world over. We walked past a whole range of enterprises opening onto the street – hairdressers, mini shops, car parts and, most striking of all, one which involved the burning, scraping and boiling of sheep's heads prior to sale.

Our final visit was to a youth project in which Gqwetha Gladstone was involved. It was held in a garage and was focused on welly-boot dancing – a tradition originally started by the miners in their spare time for their own entertainment. Children are attracted off the street to learn and enjoy the stamping, shouting and exuberant dancing. The children, aged from five to sixteen, mostly learn from each other and invent their own routines, and an outside stage enables them to perform on site. They are also now able increasingly to perform in other parts of the city. We sat in the garage and formed a delighted audience of four elderly Brits outnumbered by swarms of young children, on the floor and on our laps. The project is called Happy Feet.

What a day! Our eyes and hearts were opened and more than once our mouths gaped.

Part III

Rainbow Signs

'A rainbow nation at peace with itself and the world'

President Nelson Mandela

'The Rainbow People of God'

Archbishop Desmond Tutu

Ladies at Work

We first visited Dalukhanyo Pre-School in November 2010 with a Riviera tour party. The children, aged three upwards, danced and sang for us. We were moved by their energy, joy and friendliness, in conditions of such relative poverty. That evening we agreed that we could do better for those kids than 'just put money into a box', the idea of the Langa Township Pre-School Trust was formed and the trust deed was signed the following February. Since then there have been four more visits to Cape Town and the work of our trust is fully covered at www.langapreschooltrust.uk.

The Dalukhanyo Pre-School in Langa Township is one of a number of self-help projects, including a number of pre-schools in several townships, arising from the black empowerment movement in the 1980s and the associated mid-1980s hostels movement. The start and progress of the pre-schools initiative owes much to the dedication and hard work of a number of women, and this tells the story of some of the women who have made the Dalukhanyo and Nomonde pre-schools happen.

Yolisa

It is important to start with the life and continuing invaluable voluntary contribution of Yolisa Gqirana; this story is based on notes written by Yolisa about her life and some interviews with her and some of her friends in Langa Township.

Yolisa was born a Xhosa in April 1955 in Stutterheim in Eastern Cape Province. She had one brother and four sisters. Her father was very cruel but died when she was still a young girl. She feels that this experience made her stronger and more self-sufficient.

She grew up a member of the Presbyterian Church. She was educated at two schools and especially enjoyed sport and singing. As a young girl she had a baby boy and she feels that she let her mother down at that time, but her mother loved and raised that son. The boy's father died in 2008.

Her mother allowed her to come to Cape Town to assist an elder sister in her business in 1980. Yolisa lived illegally in a men's hostel, illegal because she had no pass and because she should not have been in that hostel. She became secretary for a weekly meeting of hostel women. It was a time of great stress for Yolisa as the police were rigidly enforcing the apartheid laws by apprehending people early in the morning each day, apart from Saturdays and Sundays! Those without passes were sent back to Eastern Cape if they were Transkei people, whilst the Ciskei people were sent to prison, from which they would be released if relatives paid a fine or were able to present their passbooks.

Yolisa typifies the way people were living, and the possible dire effects, in her statement on 'A Woman's Life in a Hostel for Men', delivered in 1991 at a training centre:

Let me draw a picture of the hostel where I stay. It is like a long carriage divided into six rooms. In each and every room there are three beds. Each bed accommodates one family. There is one entrance/hallway which serves as the dining room and kitchen for the whole hostel. You have to stay in this kitchen with your food while it cooks for fear of someone stealing it or removing it before it is ready. Father, mother, child share the single bed, while the older children sleep on the floor like sardines. Imagine for yourself what it must be like.

If you get visitors then they too must be accommodated in the same bed. Children hear all the whispers of the parents. The most difficult time for women is when they wash themselves. The rooms are always occupied by men and the only secretive place is the toilet and that is always busy. It is difficult to keep the children clean. The toilet is a makeshift one that every morning has a long queue. You could never send a child to the toilet on her/his own because there is no seat and they could drown and because the floor is always wet and they could slip badly. You will never succeed in training your child in cleanliness. They often play in the sand, but the sand itself is not clean because the drinkers spit all over it. There is a lot of child abuse in these places so you can never be sure your child is safe. It is common for the children to get into fights and get hurt. Also the intoxicated people get into fights themselves and then they trample the children to show their greatness. But at last these fears are vanishing. This is due to the opening of the pre-school – thanks to the hostel dwellers' own association. The children are very keen to attend these pre-schools because they are safe from beatings and sexual abuse. In these hostels you will find that the women are the ones making a living. They do that by selling liquor, vegetables or anything else that will bring a little money in.

During Yolisa's time in Langa, from 1983/84 onwards, a succession of organisations was being formed, merging, and leading and influencing events in some of the townships. Yolisa mentions that the initiative came from migratory workers (the Amasoka, or Huis Toegaan in Afrikaans), particularly in the townships of Langa, Nyanga and Gugulethu. She writes that the aims were 'to fight against the Apartheid Pass laws, against torturing people when they were doing their businesses, and fight for themselves to show that they are not single, they've got families and they will stay with their families'. Particular work included the hostels to home development, mobile clinics and child care, a women's group and a youth group.

A major change to the life of Yolisa came when the chairman of the Hostel Dwellers' Association, Mr Clarence Mahamba, and Sister Nosakhelle Balfour approached Mary Savage of the Early Learning Resources Unit (ELRU) to talk about how the young children could be kept safe. It was decided that two people should be sent away to be trained by the ELRU so that they could become community pre-school motivators. Yolisa from the women's group and Thobeka Mbalo from the mobile clinic were chosen. On their return they initiated playgroups in Langa, Gugulethu and Nyanga. As time went by their programme was in such demand that they pressed for the capacity to run a number of pre-schools over long periods each day. By the time the Umzamo Development Project took over the work of the Hostel Dwellers' Association, Yolisa was visiting seven pre-schools in three townships, conducting workshops for teachers and parents and educating them about child care.

Concerning the Dalukhanyo Pre-School, Yolisa writes that Joyce Ndlwana and Lillian, the current principal and deputy, joined in 1991 and they earned Rand 40 per month; 'we were not charging parents any fees because we needed to make them understand what is child care by workshops, meetings and other creative ways'. As founders of the pre-school they supported the teachers by fundraising, training, even getting them to cook for the children.

Now, over twenty years later, Yolisa is proud that the venture is sustainable. However, there was a setback when in 1999 the Housing and Pre-School Development Project organisation closed down for financial reasons and Yolisa lost her job. The teachers at the Dalukhanyo and Nomonde pre-schools visited her and Mr Mahamba, asking for help to make their work sustainable. There followed a time of hard work, fundraising, encouraging tourists to visit Dalukhanyo, getting extra buildings and finding staff to work as volunteers to meet the needs of a growing number of children.

From 2001 to 2002 Yolisa worked at the University of Cape Town as an administrator in the finance department. Her contract ending in March, from September that year until 2004 she worked as a cashier in the Cape Town Swimming Pool. Her next and latest employment has been on a one-year rolling contract with St John's Ambulance as a home-based carer. During all these years Yolisa, whatever her other work, has continued to give her time, her love, her administration and her leadership to the Dalukhanyo Pre-School and to other pre-school initiatives including the Nomonde Pre-School.

Yolisa introduced me to three ladies who had also been pivotal to the establishment of pre-schools in Langa Township. These were Joyce and Lillian, respectively the principal and deputy principal of Dalukhanyo, and Ruth Lumka, the principal at Nomonde.

Born in Eastern Cape in 1960, Joyce came to Langa to live with her cousin after the pass laws were abolished in 1985, so she had no problems with the police. For several years she minded children but in 1991 she became heavily involved in setting up the embryonic Dalukhanyo, open-air play groups for children on some

Joyce

barren land, which is now occupied by the Dalukhanyo buildings. Asking how they managed in bad weather, I was told that they had the permission of hostel dwellers to use their nearby buildings when necessary, as they were empty during the day. Given some scepticism in the community about this initiative, Joyce and Lillian went out into the community, finding children and talking to their parents.

Lillian had come first to Langa, again without a passbook. She stayed for a few years brewing calabash, finally to be apprehended by the police, sent to prison and then transferred back to the Eastern Cape, where she had been brought up. She returned later and became involved with the playgroup movement.

Joyce and Lillian, working at the Dalukhanyo Pre-School for twenty-four years, have seen it grow from outdoor playgroups to classes in abandoned and requisitioned containers, which were replaced in 2005, and now to 150 children aged six months to six years of age in several year groups, with trained volunteer teachers and occupying increasingly better buildings and conditions. Staff from the local junior schools taking Dalukhanyo children have commented favourably on the liveliness and good behaviour of the children, and their skills in numbers, writing, colour and shapes. Similar compliments are given to Ruth Lumka about her children from the Nomonde Pre-School.

Ruth is very interesting, having come to Langa without a passbook in 1971. Asked if she saw herself as illegal at that time, she replied firmly, 'I had no pass, but I am supposed to be here because it is my country.' Having been involved with playgroups from 1983 onwards, Ruth later trained. She and Yolisa and others took over what was to be the Nomonde site in 1991, as bulldozers cleared away some shacks, and made sure that it was fully understood that this space was going to be occupied and used for the children of Langa, come what may.

The long experience of Yolisa within the community, going back three years, her fluency in English, her range of skills, her deep commitment to the children and staff make her an invaluable asset. We have found her full of ideas as to what is needed for the future, and it is a stimulant and a pleasure to liaise with her as our trust works to support pre-schooling in Langa Township. She is surrounded by women who work in the pre-schools and guided by a local committee chaired by Clarence Mahamba, her constantly available, elderly mentor and confidante.

Micro-farming in the Cape Townships

⌒⌒⌒

As two trustees of the Langa Township Pre-School Trust (LTPT) we first met Harvest of Hope in November 2010, when we visited the headquarters at Abalimi Bezekhaya (AB – Farmers of Hope) in Philippi, on the Cape Flats, about 15 kilometres from the centre of Cape Town. Additionally there are two non-profit garden centres and nurseries in Khayelitsha and Nyanga. The Philippi headquarters covers a site of 12 hectares and is a complex of buildings previously used for making pre-cast concrete beams.

Harvest of Hope, set up by AB, is the first short food chain community-supported agriculture scheme in South Africa, and a model for similar initiatives. It offers regular income security to micro-farmers by contracting them to grow seasonal organic produce at a guaranteed price. Customers sign up and pay at least three months in advance, which is an excellent basis for stable planning and security for the farmers. It is these farmers who weekly come to Philippi with their produce.

The day we visited was a Tuesday, the pivotal day in the weekly routine when produce from the micro-farms is brought to the central sorting and packing shed. The vegetables are picked from 6.30 in the morning, collected by the drivers, sorted by weight and quality, and ready for packing by 10.30. Later the drivers deliver the boxes to twenty-three collection points for further distribution.

When we visited, a dozen or more people, a mixture of micro-farmers and volunteers, were working around a long line of tables, heaping together and sorting the cabbages and the carrots, the onions and the sweet potatoes, the lettuces and tomatoes, the rhubarb and whatever else had been brought in for sorting. The next job was to pack boxes, large and medium, preparing for distribution to customers around Cape Town later in the day. The shed was a hive of activity in a quietly determined and happy atmosphere, which we were greatly impressed by.

We wanted to learn more and have visited the centre and gardens several times since then, and we have read a lot! A special result of this

Harvest of Hope Tuesday shed

first visit was our decision that LTPT should support the work by buying a weekly supply of vegetables to help feed pre-school children in Langa Township in the Dalukhanyo Pre-School, a scheme extended in 2014 to the Nomonde Pre-School.

Whilst welcoming the subsistence basis of the work we knew that the sale of surplus vegetables would have what economists call the 'multiplier effect'. An initial expenditure leads to earnings; such earnings are spent, to become the earnings of other people, who also then spend to the benefit of others, and so the cycle of earning and spending rolls on. In this whole cycle there is also some saving which leads to more invest-ment, widening the multiplier effect and promoting development to the good of all involved.

Abalimi Bezekhaya, founded in 1982/83 by Christina Kaba and Rob Small, is a community-based citizen sector organisation registered as a non-profit organisation with the Department of Social Development. It is working to improve sustainable food production and nature conservation through establishing and nurturing organic micro-farms amongst the poor in Cape Town. The focus is on skills development, through training and supporting people and organisations wishing to practise organic micro-farming and to promote sustainable development. The micro-farmers grow vegetables and other foods in home gardens, community gardens and small farms, work which can transform a barren area.

A micro-farm is defined by AB as anything from a 100-metre square home garden up to a one-hectare community garden. In October 2015 the farmer register included nearly 5,800 family micro-farmers, which includes around 500 micro-farmers in a hundred community garden projects. AB reckons that it has around 70–100 community gardens intensively worked at any one time. Its farmer register is growing at the rate of 1000 names annually. Recent research shows that 75% of the farmers are active at any one time.

Before and after

Concerning the number of people eating the produce, the first point is the self-sufficiency of the families involved, and the estimate is that 29,000 people eat fresh vegetables from their family micro-farms. Unknown is the amount of food given to neighbours and friends. Additionally an important proportion of the food grown is packed into the boxes for sale on a weekly basis to customers including many individual families in better-off parts of Cape Town and a few schools, old folks' day centres and hospitals. Of the R2,000,000 earned annually, half goes back to the farmer and half is retained to support training and buy equipment, seeds and fertilisers.

Currently an average of 450 boxes are provided weekly, fifteen of which are purchased by our Langa Township Pre-School Trust to be delivered to the Dalukhanyo and Nomonde pre-schools in Langa, thereby feeding daily up to 240 children. In March 2014 the Dalukhanyo cook, Nonzukiso Kiva, whilst overseeing her daily cauldron of soup, told us about children joining the pre-school for first time who, suffering from malnutrition, benefit within a month from their new, regular daily diet.

The whole AB operation is administered by a core full-time staff of seventeen supported by contracted or casual staff of around fourteen. The majority of the core staff have been farmers drawn from the target group, and they are largely women, mothers and grandmothers. The 'target group' are the poor, unemployed and disadvantaged and from these ranks come the people who are desperate to improve their lot. The experienced AB workers also represent whole families which benefit and they bring their experience, their enthusiasm and their earnings back into the townships to help others. There is strong support from volunteers, both organisations and individuals, ranging from nine to twenty at any one time, coming not only from Cape Town but more widely from South Africa and from places abroad including Denmark, Germany, the Netherlands, the USA, the UK and Sweden.

Who are the micro-farmers? This question is answered succinctly by AB in one of its publications:

> The community-garden micro-farming groups are typically made up of 3 to 8 farmers. Most of the growers are women – pillars of strength in their families and neighbourhoods. But more and more men are getting involved as they see opportunities for making a decent, dignified and sustainable living out of peri-urban farming. Typically the farm plots are the size of a few classrooms and are often located on pieces of land at schools and in Townships or on council land. In order to supply their vegetables to the Harvest of Hope box scheme, the micro-farmers need to have achieved high levels of quality and need to be farming according to strict organic principles. Training and support from Abalimi is helping to bring more eligible micro-farmers into the Harvest of Hope supply chain.

It is very moving to read the stories of the people who are benefiting from an initiative which finds a person who finds a plot of land, who goes on a training course, who is supplied with materials and knowledge, and whose life is then transformed along with those others in the family and neighbourhood. For example, Nowetu Mbekeni said in 2013:

> Abalimi has taught me to do everything that a garden needs: fencing, watering, fixing the soil and growing own seedlings. My parents were also farmers, so we were born with the talent to grow. We have to keep on doing it. The garden is my baby. My day is not complete without going to the garden. Sometimes I just walk between the plots and look at the plants. I have the feeling that they talk back to me ... It is also about changing your points of view. Many people think that they need a big piece of land. Now I know that you can plant everywhere: in bottles, tyres and bags. But I am still going on with the training and I want to learn more. There is always space for improvement.

Whilst Nokuntu Zamkana said:

> Now I know how to prepare the soil for light, medium and heavy feeders. I've also learned the planting calendar, when to plant which crop according to the seasons ... Apart from earning money through the micro-farm it also does a lot for me as a person. When I'm walking through the garden it makes me happy. I am feeling proud when people are watching me work in my garden. I feel important because people ask me about my plants and admire them.

These stories bring us to a particular challenge for micro-farming in the area, which is the nature of the soils. The Cape Flats consist largely of unconsolidated Aeolian sands, wind-blown from the beaches over the centuries and deposited as sheets and dunes. The resulting soils are acidic and, naturally hostile to cultivation, can only be worked using scientific methods and patient care. AB faces the difficulties of developing and supporting hundreds of potential micro-farmers as they tackle these soil conditions and cope with the demanding weather conditions, the seasonal fluctuations, the periods of drought, the difficult winds, the scorching sun and sometimes driving rain and floods.

Basic to the work of AB are the principles of scientific farming, sustainable development, land conservation and community involvement. Soils are improved through the introduction of organic waste and worms, and special care is taken with water conservation. Trees and shrubs are being planted through community greening projects to protect plots from damaging winds. They are also planted to protect and enhance places such as edu-care centres, churches, schools, and health and community centres. There are initiatives to use biomass to produce methane gas, which is used for distributing water and boiling and cooking, whilst solar panels are in evidence, the electricity helping to distribute the water on some plots. An excellent example is at the Siyazama Community Allotment Garden Association in Khayelitsha, which is on municipal commonage under some power lines. Here there are thirteen micro-farmers, the leader being Nokwanda Nkqayi. Here a biomass unit fed by fresh garden waste produces methane gas, which is pumped by solar energy into a stove inside the kitchen of the thatched building used by the micro-farmers for visitors, meetings and meals.

Abalimi indicates that the foundation of the micro-farming movement has been the 'survivalist and subsistence' gardeners, who have been guided into the urban organic farming culture. The skills learnt are there for a lifetime and can be used when there is no employment or to supplement wages. It is estimated that it costs R50 (say £2.50) to establish a door-sized garden and R3,900 (say £200) for a viable 100m² organic household garden. Abalimi provides training bursaries and inputs subsidies to poor households, from which the majority of the micro-farmers come. Bigger initiatives are the community-driven gardens in school grounds and on council land, ranging in size from 1,000 square metres to one hectare. Quoting from the AB Overview of April 2014:

> ABALIMI offers support with planning, capital developments, installation of plant and equipment, training, soil inputs, seeds and plants and follow-up over an initial three-year period ... ABALIMI-supported urban organic community gardens are the first to have proven that permanent livelihoods can be created on micro-farms, while conserving and promoting indigenous flora and fauna. A 1000m² community garden to set up currently costs approximately R100 000 [circa £5000] over three years, from which a minimum of two modest family livelihoods can be created.

The widening reach and influence of AB is shown by the number of independent and associated initiatives born or nurtured in Abalimi. These include the Manyanani Peace Park, the Siyazama Allotment Garden Association and also the Moya we Khaya Peace Gardens at Khayelitsha, the Schools Environmental Education and Development Programme, the Vukuzenzele Urban Farmers Association, and the Farm and National Garden Trust. Each initiative has its own purpose and history, but there are common features: the involvement of people of all ages in local development, the emphasis on local food production and job creation, the importance of environmental education and training, and the financial support of Cape Town and national government and various foundations and individuals. The key foundation of all of this, however, is Abalimi acting as a catalyst, a leader, a manager and a demonstration project.

Co-operation in the Winelands

❦

It is said that the South African wine industry is the eighth largest in the world and it is particularly famous for its Chenin Blanc, Pinotage and Shiraz. Interest in this story started during a visit in February 2014 to the Solms-Delta vineyard and museum in the Drakenstein Valley near Franschhoek. The visit had coincided with a series of articles and letters to the press, which focused on social problems in the vineyards and effects on children arising from the Dop, the previously prevalent wine-for-work system. Yet at Delta we found a well-run place with delightful staff, outgoing, helpful and happy. During a brief wine-tasting a waitress even sang to us in a charming way. We were very impressed by the whole atmosphere and by the museum that had been established.

The Museum van de Caab tells the story of the area where the Delta farm is, starting with the earliest known human activity and running through pre-colonial pastoralism to private ownership and the development of viticulture. The museum traces this local history in the wider context of development in the Cape region. The times and lives of the earliest people in the area, tracing back 7,000 years, and of the San and Khoekhoe groups are described; also covered is the extent of their assimilation, and that of slaves brought in from India, the East Indies, Madagascar and elsewhere, within the colonial and post-colonial economies and culture. The special emphases of the museum include fine displays on the first proven inhabitants during the Late Stone Age, the San hunter-gatherers, and the Khoekhoe pastoralists who fought two wars against the Dutch settlers in the late seventeenth century, as they clashed with the Trekboers over grazing and water rights. We learn about the earliest European settlers, and particular stories about the Delta farm, its establishment, its reliance on slave labour, sexual relations between masters and slaves and the inevitable emergence of the coloured community. Slavery, emancipation, the rise and fall of the Cape wine industry in the nineteenth century, the pre-apartheid discriminatory racial policies and attitudes, the apartheid era, the liberation movement and the post-1994 democratic period are all covered.

The museum story is based on the Delta farm, its people and the times they lived through in the wider context of the march of history, and current workers at Solms-Delta tell their stories. This excellent museum initiative arose from Mark Solms, of the sixth generation of the family occupying Delta for 320 years. In an article in the *Guardian* colour supplement on Saturday 6 December 2014 Mark Solms, having been away from South Africa for a number of years, stated that he wanted to make a contribution:

> I took on this farm in 2001, which had been a private estate for 320 years, and gathered my new staff and workers. I wanted to run it in a way that is fair. The workers thought I was mad. They began to come in late or not appear on Mondays. Everything fell apart. I realised I was taking on the whole history of South Africa. My ancestors took their farms for themselves. It destroyed the local economy and worse, there was genocide. I was taking that legacy. I knew people like me should give the land back, but I couldn't do it. Instead I mortgaged the land and bought the farm next door, so the workers could own that land. We now have three farms as part of a trust combined into one enterprise. Each of us – me, my partner and the workers as a group – have one third of that. The mood on the farm is transformed. It's like living in a village. We have very good wages, there's a farm workers' committee and we started a pre-school on the farm.

Solms-Delta vineyard

To explain in greater detail, Mark Solms, having taken over the farm, indicated the intention to introduce land reforms and in 2005 the Solms family established the Wijn de Caab Trust, 'the mission of which is to break the cycle of poverty and dependency among historically disadvantaged tenants and employees on the Delta-Solms Estate', of which there are 200. He also persuaded a friend, Richard Astor, to buy an adjacent farm to increase the estate's development capital. Then Solms and Astor put up their two farms as collateral so that a third neighbouring farm could be purchased by the workers. By this means the trust has a third equity share in Solms-Delta (Pty) Ltd, and the related profits from wine sales are used to benefit the workers and their families. This means better housing for them, and the provision of health and educational support and also recreational and other leisure facilities. To quote from the aerial view of Delta in the museum's excellent publication reviewing the whole exhibition, 'The Wijn de Caab Trust therefore is an equal partner with the Solms and Astor families, in Solms-Delta (Pty) Ltd., which is a form of co-operative between the two owners and the workers as owners of a third of the company. Not only are the beneficiaries the historically disadvantaged residents and employees of Delta, but also the wider rural community in the Franschhoek Valley, as the influence of this initiative spreads.' The hope of Mark Solms is that 'future generations descended from the dispossessed indigenous inhabitants and slaves will be empowered to choose vocations on the basis of their interests and abilities rather than fate or necessity'.

In 2007 the Astor and Solms families established another trust, the Delta Trust, which 'aims to contribute to nation-building on a local scale, focusing first on the Franschhoek Valley, and more broadly the Cape Winelands. Its mission is to contribute to greater social cohesion and inclusiveness in South African communities through careful, patient and creative local cultural work.' One of its recent initiatives has been to encourage an interest in music. Solms-Delta has a choir, an eighty-person band, and two music groups. These provide a programme of musical events available to the whole of the Franschhoek Valley and more widely.

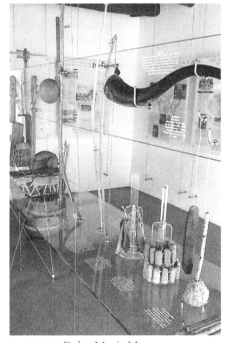

Following careful research, including interviews with some of the workers, a decision was made to establish a small 'Music van Delta' museum. In this there is a fascinating display of instruments and detailed description of the ways by which music was able to

Delta Music Museum

bridge the gaps between races and classes, to bring joy and comfort and to establish protest.

One great example refers to David Kramer, a white South African rock legend, who released his first album, *BAKGAT!*, in 1980, for it to be immediately banned by the South African Broadcasting Company. Its political satire, coarse language and mixing of languages, for example Cape Afrikaans and South African English, were unacceptable to the authorities, who did not want a fusion of music across the races. To quote from the display, 'despite such absurd efforts, music often created moments that crossed apartheid boundaries. There is something inherent in music and its enjoyment that brings people together' and 'the cross fertilisation of musics went on'.

Professor Pumla Gobodo-Madikizela of Cape Town University, in talking to journalist Crystal Orderson, is reported as saying that Solms-Delta:

> illustrates the essence of transformative dialogue, a principled commitment to a communal ethic based on values embodied within a framework of responsibility for the other. Such a framework requires a process of moral imagination, a certain intentional openness to the possibility of reaching beyond the self and towards the other.

It is interesting, therefore, to turn elsewhere for commentary. Susan Levine, in her 2013 book *Children of a Bitter Harvest*, following research started in 1998, presents several dozen case studies of the lives of children working in the Winelands, which it is proper to refer to in the light of the Solms-Delta initiatives. The studies reveal the plight and the dilemmas of these children, caught between the need to work to support parents, siblings and themselves, and the desire both to learn and to improve their lives. They are caught in a circle of circumstances, which is very difficult to break away from.

The author features examples of exploitation, bullying, arbitrary sacking, seemingly endemic in some areas, and far away from the experience of the Delta-Solms employees. Yet she is well aware that efforts to right the situation can have unexpected and unforeseen consequences. We met this in attending an agricultural fair in Stellenbosch in November 2012 where the big emphasis was on new equipment and systems to save labour in the vineyards. This was the very time at which poor rural people in the Western Cape were protesting about low wages. In November 2012 and in the following January, national highways were barricaded with burning tyres in protest and some vineyards were damaged. The connections between the cost of labour and the benefits of mechanisation to replace labour are legion in the history of humankind!

In his foreword to Levine's book, the analysis of Professor Andries du Toit of the University of the Western Cape is devastating. He refers to the work of Elizabeth Povinelli in 1980 as follows:

> [O]ne of the most remarkable aspects of this moment in history is the way in which, within the charmed circle of the lives of the privileged and well-resourced, the unequal distribution of hope and harm, of endurance and exhaustion, is made to appear not only sensible but inevitable, but also ... the ideologies of present-day liberal societies work to make the unpalatable facts of late capitalism acceptable.

I sense that in the hard-driving and individualistic neoliberal world of these days it is expected that market forces will resolve all the problems, given time, and in the meantime the disenfranchised and the poor inevitably must suffer. The aim is for government to do less and cost less and for untrammelled market forces to prevail. It brings me to reflect that during the nineteenth-century free trade experiments of the British governments, grain was exported from south-eastern Ireland whilst hundreds of thousands elsewhere in Ireland died in the Great Potato Famine of 1845. Free trade philosophy prevented top decision makers from intervening until it was too late to prevent the decimation of large parts of rural Ireland.

Professor du Toit feels that the increasingly hard-pressed farmers in Western Cape are somewhat at the mercy of supermarkets in the northern hemisphere. From my experience in the UK I would say rather that it is an increasingly well-informed public shopping around for the 'best buy' in the face of huge competition between the world's wine growing regions, to get the best deals from Tesco, Sainsbury's, Aldi, Lidl, the Co-op and the like. A current Aldi slogan is 'Award-winning wines for less', coupled with the line 'Spend a little, live a lot'. Our UK dairy farmers face the same problem as South African vine growers: the competition between supermarkets to get the 'best deal' for their customers. Whilst the ILO can indicate the ideal minimum wage or a fair wage, merciless competition will lead to corners being cut and to mechanisation.

Answers may rest, therefore, in the sort of pragmatic and ethical approach adopted at Solms-Delta, in worker co-operatives and the increase in fair trade initiatives supported by an increasingly discerning public, and in a focus on quality. The last point was well made by Eben Sadie of the Sadie Family vineyards in Swartland, reported by Matt Goulding in 'Roads and Kingdoms', in his view that emphasis should be on quality, concentrating on the *terroir*, thereby enabling higher prices to be paid to the vineyard and the vintner. Quoting from 'Roads and Kingdoms', I conclude with Sadie's pithy comments:

> If you sell a 29 Rand bottle, the government takes R 5.10, the supermarket makes a killing, and the property makes 36 cents. With that money the grower has to maintain his equipment, replant, improve and try to go forward. There are no subsidies ... while the small farmers themselves are barely hanging in, the supermarkets are negotiating for more productivity and lower prices.

Social Responsibility Initiatives and Charities

∽෨෩

Our experience in Cape Town has given us an appreciation of the dedicated work of local people, often significantly helped by foreign funding and technical advice, to educate and to alleviate poverty, and to involve the less privileged and unprivileged in both subsistence and paid work. Whilst major local initiatives have been referred to earlier in the stories 'An Unsung Hero', 'Ladies at Work', 'Micro-farming in the Cape Townships' and 'Co-operation in the Winelands', the following pieces, of varying lengths, are written to illustrate the diversity of the very encouraging initiatives we have met, both large and small scale, at work to alleviate poverty and to support personal development.

The important common feature of all of these initiatives is that they have depended on leadership, on people with a vision and a hope for the future. These are people with the ability to cause things to be done through their belief that things can change. Such people are from all walks of life and with very varying educational, ethnic and social backgrounds.

Of varying contributions, even taken together, these activities seem to be a drop in the ocean in the face of the huge problems, but, as Mother Teresa put it, 'We ourselves feel that what we are doing is just a drop in the ocean. But the ocean would be less because of that missing drop.' It is greatly encouraging also to see the pivotal support, both through finance and through voluntary work, which arises from abroad for some of these initiatives.

Masicorp in Masiphumelele Township

This densely crowded township of 40,000 people is 40 kilometres to the south of Cape Town. It is occupied largely by Xhosa-speaking immigrants from the Eastern Cape Province. Most of them live in one-roomed shacks, sometimes with up to six people in each. Electricity is available, but water is carried from stand pipes and communal toilets are each shared by about sixty adults and children. Only about 30% of the people are in regular employment, generally in unskilled work. There are problems with drug-related crime, domestic violence and sexual abuse. HIV/AIDS affects about 25% of the population and life expectancy is fifty.

This is the background to the very significant contribution being made to this community by Masicorp, which has been working in the township since 1999. Masicorp is a small community-based non-governmental organisation. It was founded by John and Carol Thompson from the USA, and has two full-time staff and over sixty volunteers. Funding comes from the USA and Europe, as well as from South African sources. The slogan of Masicorp is 'Partners in education and enterprise' and it has a diverse and growing programme of activities vital to this community. The mission is 'to work with the people of Masiphumelele and key partners, offering opportunities, through education and enterprise, to help themselves out of poverty towards a sustainable livelihood'.

I visited the township on 22 October 2015, meeting Milli Firth and Fiona Maitland, the two full-time administrators of Masicorp, in the adjacent garden centre for a briefing. It so happened that this day was one of peace, having been preceded by several days of riots, problems which continued the next day and through to the following week. In brief, two men accused of rape and murder had been shot; two others had fled. The seeming leader of the 'vigilantes' had been arrested, and efforts were being made to find and release him, to the extent that the police were moving him around Cape Town every four hours. Finally, in the magistrates' court in Simon's Town, surrounded by Masi people, the leader was let out on bail, which was raised by local leaders through a levy of Rand 10 on every household in Masiphumelele. Before this happened people in the township also had started to settle scores with leading drug pushers, which was causing more trouble with both the police and troops being sent in.

Back to the main story. Milli and Fiona took me into the township that Thursday to look at a very impressive pre-school development and I met the project manager, Clarence Kenny, who will now help us at the Dalukhanyo Pre-School in Langa. Milli, driving us back along the narrow lane between shacks, turned a corner to find the way blocked by a large vehicle. The speed and determination with which Milli reversed round the corner and back up the lane reminded me of an American cops and robbers movie.

The wide range of Masicorp's work is highly focused, special and inspirational. To quote from the summary, in relation to their vision for the township, 'everyone will have access to quality education, training, advice and support'. Their current projects include: continuing support for the community library and the attached learning support centre, which they have built and bequeathed; the Seedlings project supporting four pre-schools, with a training programme for principals and staff, and feeding over 700 children; at Ukhanyo Primary School, teacher training and support in English and science, physical education coaching and equipment, a classroom makeover project and school management support; at the high school, a maths and science Saturday club supporting 120 students; twenty-two students in their university bursary programme, with forty supported students having previously graduated; 'English ... please!', an English language and literacy programme for thirty of the township children who are pupils at the nearby Fish Hoek Primary School; and finally the Evangeline women's life skills programme, run annually for forty-eight women, many affected by HIV/AIDS, to give them a better chance of finding work and supporting their families.

It is impressive and moving to see all their work and it is a model for many of us.

Lutheran Community Centre (iThemba Labantu) in Philippi

Philippi is a township largely of shacks and inhabited mostly by migrants from the Eastern Cape Province. There is extreme poverty, 90% are unemployed, AIDS is estimated to affect one third of the population and the murder rate in the Philippi police district is the highest in South Africa. This is the background to the work of a church-based NGO to help the severely disadvantaged people of this township, 40 kilometres from Cape Town, covering an area from which white farmers were removed when apartheid had declared the area to be 'black'.

The Lutheran church left behind was bought up by the Moravian Church and two Lutheran churches, and a trust was formed to establish the centre. There is a staff of eighteen, including a manager, four nurses, eight carers, two cooks, two volunteers and a driver. The aim is to show God's love through their actions and to improve social and economic conditions by offering free access to nutrition, education and health care. The aim also is to empower people through income-generating and skills development projects and through recreational and team-building projects. The projects include health, adult and youth education, nutrition, income-generation programmes and leisure activities. There has been important financial support from German, South African and Norwegian organisations, which has helped to establish infrastructure and support staff and supplies. The important range of projects has been developed over the past twelve years.

The pre-school currently has forty children and concentration is on life skills, personality, nutrition and English; breakfast and lunch are supplied. There is also the important morning class, where the focus is on children aged seven to twelve with no birth certificates or IDs, this having prevented them from enrolling in state schools. The aim is to get their education started and to establish paperwork so that they can get into full-time education.

On the adult education side there are three initiatives. Opened in 2007, there is the Computer Training Centre with eighteen computers and an attendance of 250; a well-staffed and well-equipped Motor Mechanics Training Centre, opened in 2009, is able to train up to ten apprentices, and also opened in 2009 was the Solar Technician Training Centre with the capacity to train five apprentices at a time. These initiatives are profoundly important to the participants, giving them the opportunity to get employment.

For adults there are three income-generating projects: beading, the making of bags and, since 2009, ceramics. The first two of these are particularly vulnerable depending on varying demand, whilst the third is well supported by custom from Germany, Sweden and the USA.

The Care Centre is another special contribution. The background is the estimated 30% of people with AIDS. Within the centre there is a unit with the capacity to care for twenty patients and the special point is made that, with treatment, including antiretroviral treatment, there are some remarkable recoveries. Patients come in, seemingly at death's door, starving and poorly cared for, but with love, food and attention, later 'they get up, take their bed and walk'. However, some patients are in the third and fourth stages of the illness and there is a separate hospice in the Care Centre able to take five male and five female patients who, with care, are able to die with dignity.

The centre is also an active community building, supporting and leading a number of leisure activities. The gym club, formed in 2001, has over fifty regular attendees and is successful in country-wide competitions. The football club has four coaches and six age groups each of about twenty players. Coaching is every afternoon, the aim being to involve the children in activities and keep them off the street. The karate project involves thirty young people, aged seven to eighteen, being coached to gain physical and mental fitness. The marimba band project enables children to play musical instruments and keeps them in touch with their heritage, although much more could be achieved for more children if the resources were available. Finally there is the Siyaphambili (Xhosa for 'we are going forward') drama project, aimed at children and adults within the age range of six to twenty-five. There are drama, puppet, dance and theatre workshops. There have been successful and award-winning performances, but shortage of funds to travel reduces the possibilities for the performers to compete and to prove themselves in a wider circle, which would be needed for them to make some sort of career progress.

Langa Township Pre-School Trust (LTPT)

This trust was established in February 2011, following a November 2010 visit to the Langa Township. It aims 'to apply the income of the Charity in the Township of Langa, Cape Town to support the Dalukhanyo Pre-School and any other pre-school initiatives in the Township, and any related community projects'. 'Dalukhanyo' in Xhosa means 'bring light', a fitting name for a project aiming to support children and parents, giving the children a better start in life, the school motto being 'Build a child, build the nation'.

The aim of the trust is to support and encourage the local committee and pre-school workers in their efforts to help the children. Funds are raised in the UK through donations and profits on events, and 98% of the money spent each year goes to two pre-schools. All the work on administration, design and PR, accounts and auditing is a gift and no travel expenses are claimed.

In the first four years after the trust was established, Rand 600,000 were made available to the Dalukhanyo and Nomonde pre-schools. This has paid for a weekly supply of vegetables from the Harvest of Hope micro-farm project, tracksuits and fleeces and nappies, the re-equipment and furnishing of the kitchen, first-aid materials and fire extinguishers, and at the end of 2015 the trust installed steel palisade fencing for Dalukhanyo to replace a disintegrating fence. Interestingly the last of these was funded by the parents of Cheltenham College in the UK, in support of the college's rugby tour of the Cape Town area in the summer of 2013. A very challenging future project for the trust, during 2016 and 2017, is to finance new buildings on the Dalukhanyo site to replace a dilapidated wooden building, and an architect has been briefed to provide drawings. The trust has been helped greatly by the liaison work of Cape Town's Uluntu Africa, a Fairtrade-registered body involved in eco-tourism, which has adopted Dalukhanyo Pre-School as its social responsibility project.

The aim of the LTPT trustees in their work is not to limit the challenge, but to challenge the limits. At the start of their endeavours it was encouraging that Lord Boateng, formerly the British High Commissioner to the Republic of South Africa, wrote: 'I know Langa Township well. This is a deprived community, but one whose residents have to my certain knowledge huge potential. The children represent the best hope not just for South Africa but for the wider world and your work to give them a better start, is a great and worthwhile cause.'

Groundbreakers

This is an Ocean View initiative by Nadia Petersen, with her husband Clarence, who is the project manager for his company, Chronax Pty Ltd. He gives a proportion of the company's income to Nadia to support her community work based in their home in Ocean View. The aim is to help local children by taking them into their home to wash them and clean their clothes, by giving them an annual Christmas party and by introducing them to computers and information technology. Having relocated recently from their apartment in one of the forty-year-old blocks, Nadia and Clarence are extending their three-room City of Cape Town social housing bungalow to provide a dedicated room for their work for local children. Asked why she is doing this, Nadia replied that her upbringing has been so difficult that she wants to do her best to help children and this is what she feels she can do for them. Nadia has also provided material for the 'Simon's Town Forced Removals' story and she has written a moving epilogue to this book.

Happy Feet

In 2007 Siwiwe Mbinda started the Happy Feet Youth Project in Langa Township, which aims to bring the fun of gumboot dancing to needy children and to let people enjoy their enthusiastic and happy performances. Gumboot dancing was developed by South African migrant workers in the goldmines during the apartheid era. Gumboots were part of the standard outfit given to workers who faced foot-rotting, flooded conditions in undrained mines. The urge to express self through dance, and in the company of others, is a major and attractive part of the African persona. The gumboot dance, with the slapping of boots, stamping of feet and sometimes chanting in the performers' own language, is related to tribal rhythms and dances. Spreading out from the goldmines, troupes of these dancers came to perform to represent their companies. Over the decades the dance spread throughout South Africa and worldwide, and it has developed further into 'stepping', the dance created by African-American students.

Quoting from the cause profile on the GivenGain website, the Happy Feet project 'was founded in an effort to provide a safe after school environment for children ... Through Siviwe's work as a tourist guide in Langa, he saw an opportunity to further develop the mentor relationship he had with a small group of children. He paired responsible tourism and gumboots dance together as a catalyst to enable psychological and concrete benefits for the children.' A programme has been established 'which empowers the children through gumboots and traditional dance to be confident and disciplined in achieving their goals both on and off the stage'. The participants are required to balance their school work and participation in Happy Feet activities, as well as carrying themselves into the community. The programme includes approximately seventy boys and girls aged from three to twenty. Through dedication and hard work Happy Feet has performed at conferences, traditional ceremonies, hotels, universities, street parties, dance competitions, museums and in Parliament. The funding Happy Feet receives goes towards uniforms, traditional instruments, a feeding scheme, school fee and material support, and outings and functions.

The Gary Kirsten Foundation

The photograph on the next page, of a famous South African cricketer, Gary Kirsten, in a coaching session, was taken in the grounds of a high school in Khayelitsha and shows the conditions in which the young are playing their games. The sandy ground, with its sparse tufted vegetation, is part of the windblown Cape Flats, on which townships have been settled over the past sixty-five years. This is the geographical background

Gary Kirsten plays a straight bat at Khayelitsha

to the overall aim of the Gary Kirsten Foundation, through raising funds and investing, to encourage the development of cricket in townships through establishing sustainable facilities such as cricket nets and full-sized artificial cricket ovals. Also the Gary Kirsten Cricket Academy is working with the foundation to identify and empower accredited coaches who will service the needs of junior schools, high schools and cricket clubs in the surrounding township areas of Cape Town.

The specification of the cricket oval includes the artificial pitch area, a surface water drainage system, sight screens, container pavilion, score-board, boundary ropes and boards. The benefits of the facility are the 'creation of a sustainable sports ecosystem'; minimal maintenance and running costs; reduction of water, fertiliser and labour costs; reduced reliance on government and municipalities; the provision of a quality facility for local fixtures to be played. It is of critical importance that community interest should be developed and that there should be multi-purpose usage of these desperately needed multi-purpose facilities. In this way there can be the continuing development and retention of township talent and the build-up of community interest in cricket and other sports.

Trek Fishing

Our interest in this subject was sparked by a scene one afternoon along the Fish Hoek beach, with quite heavy surf being driven in by onshore winds. It was a gloriously sunny day in February 2014 and I watched as about a dozen men emerged from the sand dunes, heading for a large rowing boat. They carried two long and very stout poles, which they inserted through loops in the sides of the boat. This way, carrying the boat on their shoulders, they surged through the surf to some deeper water. Four of them clambered aboard and started rowing frantically against the surf to a spot about 300 yards out from the beach. As they rowed a thick rope played out behind them and was held by some of their mates remaining on the beach.

We watched the action, but could not understand what was going on. Clearly they were trying to catch fish and had headed to where a shoal seemed to be. They let out a net, one like a seine net, which gathers the fish in and gradually closes at the opening. Something seemed to go wrong, there was a flurry of excitement, a fisherman with a long stick seemed to be poking it vigorously into the water. Then all went quiet, and the men on the beach hauled the boat back through the surf. Expectantly I went to see the haul of fish, but none had been caught.

I had a word with 'Ben', the elderly licensed fisherman of a German background. He was disconsolate, but philosophical. A shark had got amongst the fish, eating them and dispersing them. They could do nothing, he said; 'We can't kill the sharks, but they can kill us.' He said that he was having a bad time, getting so few fish, if any, that sometimes he couldn't pay for enough petrol to drive back home, some 15 kilometres away, so he would have to walk back or hitchhike.

The next day I spoke about this to the Afrikaner selling the *Big Issue* outside the Fish Hoek shopping mall (a former long-distance lorry driver, he had fallen on bad times). He was a mine of information. This form of fishing was centuries old, but was dying out. There had been dozens of such boats operating around False Bay, including two at Fish Hoek, where now I had seen the sole survivor on that beach. He said that licences to fish in this way were now limited to those already issued; such a licence

A haul of 194 yellowfin tuna fish

could be passed on by the holder, but only to a near relative. In this way the number of licensees was being reduced through natural wastage. Moreover, each such fisherman was only allowed to go out once daily, so it was difficult for them to make enough to live. He added that the best time to fish was early in the morning, ideally on a Saturday when, if successful, there would be the biggest demand from the local restaurants. He added that the fishermen were always happy to be helped at the end of the rope as they hauled the heavy net and the catch back to the beach!

About a week later, I saw another abortive effort by the same boat crew. This time, however, there was a bit of a panic. The rope had become detached and the boat could not be hauled in. Four rowers frantically pulled on their oars, trying to control the vessel through the surf, and in one final surge on top of a high rolling wave they ended up on the beach; it was a relief for us spectators, but presumably for them it was just another day of work unrewarded. Fascinated, I started to follow the story of the fishing industry in the local press.

Moving on to a morning in October 2015, I questioned a somewhat grouchy car park attendant about the trek fishers. He was uncommunicative except for these words: 'I don't know, I don't talk to them, I don't like them; they spread all over the beach and don't care about the public.'

Trek fishermen preparing to fish

The following Sunday, in the light of the information received on our previous visit in 2014, I was amazed by the scene at the Fish Hoek beach. Two trek fishing boats were putting out to sea throughout the day, until 5 pm, and my estimate is that each would have brought in five catches. Counting, one catch was made up of 194 'yellowfins' and, being told that each fish would fetch Rand 100, I made the catch to be worth £1,000. Mind you, with four men in each boat and another fifteen working on the beach, plus the licensee, many have to share the earnings, and clearly this was an exceptionally good day. On many days there is no fishing at all and I did not see a boat go out again until the following Friday, when the three rowers had a real rock-and-roll time trying to get out through the heavy surf, very different from the placid conditions the previous Sunday.

Essentially trek fishing is very hard labour with no mechanical aids, except the wagon which takes each catch to market. The boat is pushed out through the surf, with three rowing and one steering. Around fifteen people remain on the beach for the later work. The boat goes out about 300 yards and drifts for some time. The movement seems aimless, even random, but later a restaurateur explained what was happening. High on the mountainside is a building overlooking the bay, from which a fish shoal spotter is signalling. He has a flag in each hand and moves the flags to indicate whether he sees the shoal to be to the left, to the right, or ahead or behind. The helmsman instructs the rowers accordingly – hence the short movements, and the drift and the occasional stillness of the boat, always poised as close as possible to the shoal. When a catch has been made the rowers almost frantically surge to the shore, generally well down from where the boat was launched. The ropes attached to the net having been delivered to the waiting gang of helpers, the major and very heavy work is to pull the long net in, to untangle it and fold it back onto the boat, ready for the next fishing trip, and to carry the fish to the wagon. Those responsible for the boat, meanwhile, knee-deep in the surf and now and again saturated by it, float it parallel to the beach ready to be off again into the bay. There is great interest from watchers as all this goes on, almost a festive air as the catch is sized up and examined. At one count a crowd of a hundred and more had gathered to take in the scene. A final sour note, however, came from a restaurateur that evening who saw this fishing as unfair because the fish have come close to the shore in such numbers not to feed but to mate and spawn and should be left to get on with it. There are complications in everything one looks at!

These trek fishing scenes at Fish Hoek were given a wider perspective in reading Chapter 13, 'No longer fishing', in *After the Dance* by David Robbins. The setting for the story is Lambert's Bay, 120 miles to the north-west of Cape Town, and the nearby Elandsbaai. Recently Robbins arrived at Lambert's Bay to find that around 200 subsistence fishermen were no longer fishing. This was associated with the quota system, whereby licences to fish had been given to a group of people, represented by one signature, rather than individually to all fishermen who applied, although each fisherman had given a non-returnable application fee.

If we stand back from the Lambert's Bay story, in the Eastern Cape Province the Committee NCOP Land and Marine Resources on 13 June 2011 indicated what nationally the government is trying to achieve in terms of empowering black enterprise in all stages of the fishing industry, educating the labour force, and planning for sustainable fishing stocks, by the use of quotas, by the control of poaching and by education and investment. However, Robbins' interviews in Lambert's Bay and my own experience in Paternoster, formerly a thriving fishing village in Western Cape, indicate that implementation of the policies has damaged subsistence fishing, the quota system having driven fishermen to poaching at night and to jobs such as car washing. There has been an upwelling of criticism and protest, at Paternoster and Houts Bay for example. For this reason in 2013 the controversial allocation process was said to have been suspended, 1,560 licenses in the traditional line fishing industry having been applied for and only 260 licences having been granted.

Two recent statements further indicate the seriousness of the situation and the sorts of problems to be resolved. In August 2015 on the radio Helen Zille, the Premier of the Western Cape Province, expressed concern about the twelve small Western Cape harbours, 'once thriving communities, now going backwards'. She talked about the organisational hiatus in which her government is responsible for the shore side of the ports, whilst the national government is responsible for the sea side. Lack of action by the national government to establish a joint approach to improvement is holding things back and the provincial government is going to turn to the courts to try to find a remedy. Then on 18 September the *Cape Argus* reported that the Western Cape branch of the African National Congress is petitioning the national government to review the draft policy which, if implemented, would allocate South African fishing quotas on the basis of the country's demographics. As most of the Western Cape fishermen are coloured the feeling is that the strict application of such a law, based on black empowerment, would lead to more redundancies amongst the traditional labour force. This fear seems to be confirmed in what Robbins saw in Lambert's Bay and Elandsbaai.

Our seemingly simple Fish Hoek story, therefore, has become more complicated, affected by the interplay between various levels of govern-mental responsibility, conflicts between the white, coloured and black interests and the commercial versus subsistence interests, and overall the drive to improve efficiency whilst ensuring the sustainability of the fishing stocks. Arising out of all of this there are continuing threats to the very existence of the coloured fishing communities in the Western Cape Province.

Part IV

Vignettes

Short, evocative accounts

Mont Rochelle Vineyard Hotel

⟡⟡⟡

Mhaki Maki is the young head chef at the Mont Rochelle Vineyard Hotel in Franschhoek, who is very much into nouvelle cuisine. We met him during our stay in the hotel in November 2011. A Cape Town lad, he explained that he had wanted to train to be an electrical engineer, but had found a talent for cooking and ended up at a catering college. What intrigued us was the obvious success of this young Xhosa man, with his long Afro hairstyle, and his friendly relationship as an equal with the equally young Afrikaner hotel manager, immaculate in his blue blazer and his tie.

From LTPT publication 'Journey to Western Cape and the spirit we met there', November 2011

In the Kitchen or Outside

∽∾∾

In a Greek restaurant on Cape Town's Waterfront we got talking to an Afrikaner waiter who seemed pretty cheerful about life. We asked how things in such a restaurant had changed since 1994. He looked around at the waiters and the supervisor, variously coloured and black, around us and said, 'They would be in the kitchen or outside.'

From LTPT publication 'Journey to Western Cape and the spirit we met there', November 2011

Children as Wealth

Driving back in Cape Town from a sung Eucharist at St George's Cathedral, we talked to a coloured taxi driver, probably of Indian background. Prompted by his Arsenal pennant we found that his four sons all supported Manchester United. When we commented on such a big family he replied that he also had four step-children. In reply to our thought that this was a big responsibility he said, 'Yes, but we have great wealth, every child is wealth and we have so many children.'

On another day an African waiter was very interested in where we came from, how old we were and how many children and grandchildren we had. After listening to our reply in which we mentioned our two children and eight grandchildren, smilingly he said, 'You are both wearing crowns.'

From LTPT publication 'Journey to Western Cape and the spirit we met there', November 2011

A Visit to the Langa Dompas Office

On 6 November 2012 we visited the Dompas Museum, also known as the Heritage Museum, in Langa Township. Dompas literally means 'dumb pass', and the pass had to be carried by non-white people should they be outside their designated areas. Without a dompas, and found in a white area for example, the person would be arrested and could be fined, imprisoned or deported. The museum building had been part of the security and justice system, having within it the magistrate's court room and the holding cells for those arrested and awaiting trial. This court building would have seen the trial and conviction of thousands of people over the apartheid decades.

Pam Gaddes JP

The curator of the museum is Alfred, a jovial man and a very convincing storyteller. Learning that Pam had been a magistrate in the UK, he invited her to sit at the magistrate's desk for the photo above, which also gives an idea of the displays in the museum.

Alfred talked us through the display showing the history of Langa Township and the major events, such as in 1960 when in public defiance 50,000 people burnt their passes, and also the disastrous nationwide 1976 student riots over the proposal that all black schools should use Afrikaans and English in a 50:50 mix as languages of instruction. Afrikaans was seen to be the language of the oppressor and a popular marching slogan was, 'If we must do Afrikaans, Vorster must do Zulu.'

Satnav: Yes or No?

∽⌒∾

The overnight flight from Heathrow to Cape Town yesterday took fifteen hours. A twenty-three-year-old girl had fainted and hit the back of her head somewhere over the Sahara Desert. The captain called to see if there was a doctor on board and four materialised. It was advised to put down at Lagos in Nigeria for transfer to hospital and the diversion added three hours to our journey.

Arriving at Cape Town International Airport I picked up an Avis car hire to drive to Fish Hoek. An aside – my family cannot get over that I do not use satnav. Only yesterday the question was, 'How do you manage without it?' The answer is geography, maps, signposts, instinct and a sense of direction. Nevertheless, coming out of the airport with satnav I would have saved time and money. The road sign showed east for Cape Town and west for Somerset West and Mitchell's Plain. Remembering an earlier interest in the latter I went westward!

It was a good but long drive through the Flats to the coast, but then I got the reward. It was a very special drive along the coast, with miles of yellow sandy beaches, lines of rolling breakers and quite rugged, shrub-covered sand dunes on either side of the road, all set against a brilliant, cloudless blue sky, with a backdrop of mountains. The temperatures for the early spring in Cape Town had fluctuated from 26°C at the airport to 20°C along the coast. The drive took me the long way to Muizenberg, then on to Kalk Bay and finally to Fish Hoek. What a treat it was and it would not have happened if I had taken the satnav, which had been offered by Avis at what I thought to be a really exorbitant daily rate.

18 October 2015

The Admiral

Sitting outside the Harbour Bay Restaurant in Simon's Town, in the sun, having some Chenin Blanc and a light lunch on a Cape Peninsula spring afternoon, I am watching the world go by. The restaurant is on the edge of a small bay, with a long and quite large jetty to the left and a yacht marina on the right, behind which loom naval dockyard buildings; in front of me, in the near distance, are the grey superstructures of several South African warships. Between the restaurant terrace and the short drop to the sea is a much-used public walk.

At one point my gaze settles on a remarkable sight coming towards me: a handsome, middle-aged man in the white drill uniform of a British admiral, be-medalled and covered in gold braid. Taking this in, the brain tells me that there must be an official visit to this famous South African naval base by, say, the Admiral of the British Atlantic fleet and I return to

Simon's Town Harbour

The Rolls-Royce

reveries and gazing. Then I spot that the pavilion at the end of the jetty is swathed in Union Jacks and triangular pennants and that the pennants extend all along the jetty toward the shore. Then I spot near the end of the jetty a gleaming, black 1950s Rolls-Royce complete with Union Jack on the bonnet. Mulling over all of this I decide that there must be a royal visit to Simon's Town and that the Admiral is an equerry.

Intrigued, I ask the friendly waiter, 'Is there a royal visitor here from the UK?'

'Oh, no,' he replies, 'this is a British film company; they have found that this bay is very similar to the bay which Princess Elizabeth, your Queen, came into on return from Africa to her accession in 1952, following the death of her father, George VI. They are filming here because the costs will be only a quarter of the costs in England.'

Why did I not think of this earlier?

20 October 2015

Jaeger Walk, Fish Hoek

Jaeger Walk, known to the locals as the 'cat walk', is about half a kilometre long and has many charmingly designed and variously painted stone benches. It stretches from the Fish Hoek beach café, near which the photo above was taken, around the coast towards the Sunny View Cove and railway station. It is a delightful path for strolling just above the beach, then rises past granite boulders and rock pools towards the low cliffs of Sunny View Cove, where I have an apartment in the Ocean View. Looking out from there across False Bay towards the distant mountains is very special.

It is mid-afternoon on a magnificent spring day with clear blue skies, brilliant sunshine, and at 22°C too hot for some. I look across a small inlet of the vast False Bay, from Fish Hoek towards Kalk Bay, St James and, in

Jaeger Walk

the distance, Muizenberg. I see the stretch of buildings, the railway, the road, and the sweeping sandy beaches at the foot of barren, craggy mountainsides. My concentration is on living things, however – the cormorants, the seagulls, the seals and the sense of other things in the sea, this bay on the Indian Ocean being notorious for great white sharks.

But overall what humanity moves along Jaeger Walk on this day? An answer is people together in various groups and lonely people, running, walking, strolling, even hobbling, but no jostling and no aggression. Another answer is all colours, all shapes and sizes, all ages, variously clad, some sombre, many flamboy-

Beware the sharks

ant – the rainbow nation and tourists from all over the world at leisure. How can one apply an ethnic designation? The people look 'African', 'European', 'Asian' and 'mixed' or, as they say in these parts, 'coloured'. How can we categorise and why should we arrogantly categorise? This is humanity in its being, in its transitions, its loves and pleasures, its spiritual existence and its life.

21 October 2015

Mutual Ignorance!

〜〜〜

Coming out of the Solms-Delta Vineyard after lunch on a very hot early November Friday, I turned slowly onto the M12 road to Stellenbosch. In the shade of a tree was a thin, young coloured man thumbing a lift. He caught my eye wearily, almost desperately I thought, but I accelerated away. My family have been adamant in the advice that I should not pick up strangers in South Africa. Within a few hundred yards, my conscience kicked in and I turned back and gave the young man a lift. He only wanted to go about three miles. He asked where I was from and I told him that I was going back to England the following Monday. 'Oh,' he said, 'will you be driving there in this car?' to which I could only reply, 'No, because I would have to drive all the way up through Africa, get across the Mediterranean Sea, and drive through most of Europe; I'll go to your airport and catch a plane.' He didn't reply and left the car with thanks.

6 November 2015

The King and Queen of Africa

Yesterday evening I hosted a subscription dinner in Hemel Hempstead, UK, for the Langa Township Pre-School Trust, which was attended by the Mayor and Mayoress of the Borough of Dacorum, Councillor Gbola and Mrs Carol Adeleke. The Mayor, whose birthplace is Nigeria, was talking to us about some of his recent experiences when, in full mayoral robes, he has been visiting and speaking at schools. To our hilarity he told us that on his visit to a junior school at Aldbury village, deep in our countryside, an eight-year-old boy had asked him, 'Are you the King of Africa?'

The photo above shows the Mayor and Mayoress after the Remembrance Day service in Hemel Hempstead last November.

22 January 2016

The Restaurant Manager

⚬⚭⚮

I chatted with Terry Symes during a stay at Skilpadvlei (Tortoise Valley), the very charming wine farm on the road between Stellenbosch and Kuils River. Terry has had the concession to run the restaurant since January 2015.

Of particular interest to me in this post-apartheid era was the popularity of the restaurant with its multi-racial clientele mixing very happily together. Moreover, the taking of orders, the service and the catering was by black, coloured and white people all working co-operatively together with no signs of tension. People of all ages were coming in, including families with children. Terry explained that he had introduced alongside the restaurant a play pen area for very young children and a small playground for older children. The restaurant turnover had gone up 50% over the same ten-month period in 2014. For the first time ever the owners were not subsidising the restaurant from their wine sales. Concerning its popularity, he explained that Skidpadvlei is halfway between the wealthy white Stellenbosch community and the up-and-coming mixed-race community of Kuils River.

I concluded that these happy restaurant scenes were part of the rainbow nation moving forward together on a more settled multi-racial basis. This confirmed the impressions I had been getting from the demeanour and good humour of the reception staff, the gardeners and the cleaners. It was good to have had such an experience towards the end of this three-week stay in Cape Town.

6 November 2015

Epilogues

Epilogue from Ocean View, Cape Town: Nadia Petersen

Copied verbatim from a Nadia Petersen e-mail.

This morning as I read your Simon's Town article again I was reminded that it is better to be a lover of music than politics (or to be a musician rather than a politician) ... music has a way of soothing emotions and bringing comfort to what we go through in life than whatever those in authority can decide over you ... music gives you a form of escape that in which those in authority decide over you ... one song can bring hurt up then another can give you heart to forgive where authorised decisions can have irrevocable consequences and can scar very deep ... as we grow up in this life we learn where we come from, which race we are by already been classified by laws without even knowing which or what kind of family religion race colour we are born into ... as we grow we discover this information and have to make the most of trying to understand where those that God has entrusted to us to already come to life of deep scarring ... do you blame your grandparents your parents or do you make the best of the worst possible circumstances ... I have learned early in life that you do not have to become like where you come from ... not having the ideal life I believe that I am content and appreciate the little rainbows I get every so now and then meeting people such as your self – motivating hope in a

Nadia Petersen

world of self gain and I should say spoil those of us coming from a poor background ... my view of the points you raise of the comments and the memorial places that are placed for everyone and tourist to see I myself have never seen so it is always good to know this information as to me that many can say they love you a family member a wife to a husband you to me but at the end of the day it is our actions that speaks for itself ... why keep Indians in Simon's Town based on your needs as it suits you? So I salute the decisions of the Indians to move based on that and saying in it all treating people this way is wrong ... when I see and hear that most coloureds and Africans come from a place of NO EDUCATION I can only understand why it is should we blame Apartheid or should we take responsibility for our choices but in those difficult years only those that came from an English background or spoke English could matriculate ... if you spoke Afrikaans or Xhosa you would never stand a chance that is why many patriarchs of freedom exchange their mother tongue from an early age in primary schools just so that they could make it ... these are the children that until today assist their parents in reading letters, taking up the responsibility of paying bills, going to the doctor or very area with their parents to at least understand or assist in matters of language they do not understand but today we can matriculate in our mother tongue thanks to those who fought on our behalf, yes our country is not far from being perfect but at least we should know that we are one I take away that which classify us from one another the colour the religion the race and embrace one another as an individual person ... I am a living testimony of the ripple effects of Apartheid and believe me when I say I do not even know how I am going to better my children's future when I hear their dreams and my heart breaks but do you inspire your child or do you give them the reality of life and in that killing all hope of a better future ... don't get me wrong there are truths I do share and truths I keep away, does that make me a liar or a protector yet I am only a mother who tells them the truth where I come from already knowing that I matriculated in a world of freedom but cannot get a good job do I tell them what prospects do they have or should I still hope one day it will be 'our time'? all I can say is I have hope and a song ... regardless the country regardless the race, hurting another human can never be right ...

From my heart to You Mr Gordon Gaddes. God Bless You, Kind regards, Nadia.

Postscript from *The Observer, The New Review*, Sunday 20 December 2015:

Quoting from article by Liz Hoggard in 'Faces of 2015':

> When Viola Davis gave her Emmy acceptance speech in September, it went round the world. The first black woman to win for a lead actress in a TV drama – for ABC's *How to Get Away with Murder* – Davis started her speech by quoting Harriet Tubman, the black Underground Railroad founder: 'In my mind, I see a line. And over that line, I see green fields and lovely flowers and beautiful white women with their arms stretched out to me over that line. But I can't seem to get there no how. I can't seem to get over that line.'

Epilogue:
Fergus Pickles

A s has been referred to earlier, both my brother Ben and I were fortunate enough to go on separate rugby tours to South Africa, in 2012 and 2014 respectively, while I was lucky enough to spend two months working in South Africa during my gap year. Reading back on my own account in 'Sport and Apartheid', it is clear to see a struggle in trying to comprehend and share the complex nature of racial relations in the modern rainbow nation.

The truth is, as is often the case, our pre-conceived stereotypes and expectations contain a lot of truths despite also being very wrong. As Gordon points out in his chapter about Langa, many townships nowadays contain a full range of social classes. Soweto, perhaps South

Fergus and lads relaxing

Africa's most famous township, looks in many places unrecognisable from our expectations, with tarmacked roads and running water. Indeed, it is even home to South Africa's two most popular soccer teams: Kaizer Chiefs and Orlando Pirates. However, in amongst these are areas such as Kliptown, where a corrugated shack may be a luxury, and effluent lies in the narrow alleys and walkways.

Gordon has focused, rightly, on the community initiatives that are essential in building the nation. Of particular interest in this work are the matriarchs: the 'mamas', as they are often called. Gordon has pointed out their leading roles in both the Dalukhanyo Pre-School and the Harvest of Hope project, but their presence is felt in every community initiative to be found in South Africa. Brought up in an era of stark oppression, they are inspirational. The main challenge to be found, in fact, is in transferring their determination and uplifting spirit onto the next generation.

Many South Africans nowadays rightly bemoan the blatant corruption of the ANC and President Zuma, the continuing desperate poverty in many areas, and the wide wealth gap that still exists. The story of Simon's Town reminds us just how difficult it is to reverse decades of awful prejudice. However, it is here that stories such as those of Clarence Mahamba can be of most help in remembering just how far the country has come. Throughout my work in South Africa I was fortunate to witness many examples of the kind of uplifting communal work described throughout these pages, whether in the name of Christianity, Hinduism, Ubuntu or just a belief in the creation of a new nation.

To an outsider, such as we are, the endless complexities of modern South Africa can seem baffling. Although Gordon would never presume to have provided any kind of answer to our questions about this wonderful country, I am truly astounded by the scope of this undertaking. That he has here managed to compile such a varied and detailed portrait of South Africa as he has seen it is a huge credit to him and all those who have aided him along the way, especially his wonderful wife Pam. I am filled with admiration and love, and hope you have enjoyed it as much as I have.

Bibliography and References

❦

Part I: The Apartheid Period

Apartheid

Desmond, Father Cosmas, *The Discarded People: Account of African Resettlement in South Africa*, Johannesburg: Christian Institute, 1970

Levine, Susan, *Children of a Bitter Harvest*, Cape Town: Best Red, 2013

Meredith, Martin, *The State of Africa*, 2nd Edition, Cape Town: Jonathan Ball, 2011

ubuntu.london, *Life Is Wonderful* programme booklet, 25 January 2016

Wikipedia, 'Apartheid': https://en.wikipedia.org/wiki/Apartheid, accessed 10/04/2014

District Six Forced Removals

Cape Town History and Heritage, 'District 6', 2008: http://www.capetown.at/heritage/city/district%206.htm, accessed 12/04/2014

Mabin, Alan, 'Comprehensive segregation: the origins of the Group Areas Act and its planning apparatuses', *Journal of Southern African Studies* 18(2), 1992, pp. 405–429

Noor Ebrahim, *Noor's Story: My Life in District 6*, 7th Edition, Charlesville: I M Publishing, 2009

District Six Museum displays

Torch, 3 October 1962

Simon's Town Forced Removals

Simon's Town Historical Society, *Simon's Town and the Forced Removals of the 1960s*

Simon's Town Museum displays

Faith Groups and Apartheid

Battle, Michael, *Reconciliation: The Ubuntu Theology of Desmond Tutu*, 2nd Edition, Cleveland, Ohio: Pilgrim Press, 2009

England, Frank, 'Tracing South African Anglicanism', *Bounty in Bondage*, eds. Frank England and Torquil Paterson, Johannesburg: Raven Press, 1989

Goedhals, Mandy, 'Paternalism to Partnership?', *Bounty in Bondage*, eds. Frank England and Torquil Paterson, Johannesburg: Raven Press, 1989

Lapsley, Father Michael, *Redeeming the Past: My Journey from Freedom Fighter to Healer*, Cape Town: New Holland Publishing, 2012

Loader, JA, 'Church, Theology and Change in South Africa', *South Africa: A Plural Society in Transition*, van Vuuren et al., Durban: Butterworth Publishers, 1985

Nelson Mandela, In His Own Words, 2nd Edition, London: Abacus, 2004

South Africa: Overcoming Apartheid, Building Democracy, 'Religious Faith and Anti-Apartheid Activism': http://overcomingapartheid.msu.edu/sidebar.php?id=65-258-6, accessed 15/10/2014

Truth and Reconciliation Commission, Final Report, Volume 4, Chapter 3

Welsh, Frank, *A History of South Africa*, London: HarperCollins, 1998

Sport and Apartheid

The Guardian, John Arlott column, 29 August 1968

Meredith, Martin, *The State of Africa*, 2nd Edition, Cape Town: Jonathan Ball, 2011

Oborne, Peter, *Basil D'Oliveira, Cricket & Conspiracy: The Untold Story*, 2nd Edition, London: Little, Brown, 2005

Reddy, ES, 'Sports and the liberation struggle': http://scnc.ukzn.ac.za/doc/SPORT/SPORTRAM.htm, accessed 24/10/2014

SportsPro, 'History of Sport – South Africa emerges from its dark past': http://www.sportspromedia.com/notes_and_insights/ashes_hero_doliveira _and_the_battle_against_racism_in_cricket, originally published 2009, accessed 16/10/2014

Welsh, Frank, *A History of South Africa*, London: HarperCollins, 1998

Part II: The Flats

The Cape Flats

Africapetours, 'A History of the Townships', 2013: http://www.africapetours.com/Township%20history.htm, accessed 14/06/2013

Carlin, John, *Chase Your Shadow: The Trials of Oscar Pistorius*, London: Atlantic Books, 2015

Meyer, Deon, *Dead Before Dying*, London: Hodder, 2012

Waterstreet, 'The magic of Philippi': http://www.waterstreet.co.za/philippi/the-magic-of-Philippi, accessed 09/10/2014

Wikipedia, 'Pinelands, Cape Town': https://en.wikipedia.org/wiki/Pinelands,_Cape_Town, accessed 23/11/2014

Worcester Polytechnic Institute Flood Risk Report, 'Improving Flood Risk Management in Informal Settlements in Cape Town', 13/12/2007

World Weather Online, 'Cape Town, South Africa Weather Averages': http://www.worldweatheronline.com/cape-town-weather-averages/western-cape/za.aspx, accessed 17/11/2014

Langa Township

Africapetours, 'A History of the Townships', 2013: http://www.africapetours.com/Township%20history.htm, accessed 14/06/2013

Government report, Environment and Heritage Resources Management Branch, 'Langa: Heritage Area Designation Report', February 2014

Meredith, Martin, *The State of Africa*, 2nd Edition, Cape Town: Jonathan Ball, 2011

An Unsung Hero

SE Mxokozeli, *Commemoration of Heroes from Western Cape Hostel Communities*, unpublished

Meredith, Martin, *The State of Africa*, 2nd Edition, Cape Town: Jonathan Ball, 2011

Various cuttings provided by Clarence Mahamba, including Estelle Randall, 'Hostel workers unite', *Cape Herald*, November 1985

Ladies at Work

Gqirana, Yolisa, 'A Woman's Life in a Hostel for Men', presented to a Southern African People's Dialogue on Land and Homelessness, March 1991

Part III: Rainbow Signs

Micro-farming in the Cape Townships

Abalimi Bezekhaya, Harvest of Hope publications and website: http://abalimi.org.za/key-activities/harvest-of-hope, accessed 26/10/14

Co-operation in the Winelands

Levine, Susan, *Children of a Bitter Harvest*, Cape Town: Best Red, 2013

Goulding, Matt, 'The Last Harvest: South African Vineyard Yields Much More Than Grapes', Roads and Kingdoms: http://world.time.com/2012/12/28/the-last-harvest-south-african-vineyard-yields-much-more-than-grapes, accessed 30/10/2014

Guardian colour supplement, 6 December 2014

Museum van de Caab newspaper and displays in the two Delta-Solms museums

Solms-Delta, 'Community: Contribution to Nation Building': http://www.solms-delta.co.za/community, accessed 30/10/2014

Social Responsibility Initiatives

Masicorp: Masicorp, 'Masicorp – Partners in Education and Enterprise': http://masicorp.org, accessed 10/11/2015

Lutheran Community Centre: iThemba Labantu, 'iThemba Labantu – Lutheran Community Centre': http://www.ithemba-labantu.co.za, accessed 28/10/2015

Happy Feet: GivenGain, 'Happy Feet Youth Project': https://www.givengain.com/cause/3078/about, accessed 3/12/2014

Gumboot Dancing, 'Narrative': http://dancehistorygumbootdancing.weebly.com/narrative.html, accessed 11/28/2015

Gary Kirsten Foundation: Russel Symcox e-mail, 14/01/2016

Trek Fishing

Robbins, David, *After the Dance*, Cape Town: Jonathan Ball, 2004

Part IV: Vignettes

A Visit to the Langa Dompas Office

Wikipedia, 'Soweto uprising', https://en.wikipedia.org/wiki/soweto_uprising, accessed 16/01/2016

Epilogues

Hoggard, Liz, 'Viola Davis: "We have to live our truths through our work and define ourselves in our own terms"', *The Observer*, *New Review*, 20 December 2015

Lightning Source UK Ltd.
Milton Keynes UK
UKOW07f0035190416

272531UK00007B/39/P